# THE SKINNY ON HOW TO HAVE A FAT RETIREMENT

Published by CelebrityPress®, Orlando, FL

CelebrityPress® is a registered trademark.

Printed in the United States of America.

ISBN: 978-0-9895187-3-4
LCCN: 2013945823

This publication is designed to provide accurate and authoritative information with regard to the subject matter covered. It is sold with the understanding that the publisher is not engaged in rendering legal, accounting, or other professional advice. If legal advice or other expert assistance is required, the services of a competent professional should be sought. The opinions expressed by the authors in this book are not endorsed by CelebrityPress® and are the sole responsibility of the author rendering the opinion.

Most CelebrityPress® titles are available at special quantity discounts for bulk purchases for sales promotions, premiums, fundraising, and educational use. Special versions or book excerpts can also be created to fit specific needs.

For more information, please write:

CelebrityPress®
520 N. Orlando Ave, #2
Winter Park, FL 32789
or call 1.877.261.4930

Visit us online at www.CelebrityPressPublishing.com

# THE SKINNY ON HOW TO HAVE A FAT RETIREMENT

CELEBRITY PRESS®
Winter Park, Florida

# CONTENTS

*This book is dedicated to my incredible wife Elizabeth.
She has brought in to my life, love, family, and a loyal and
honest friend. With her I have reached professional heights
I never before imagined. I also dedicate it to my two sons,
Reese and Foster, who both teach me more than I teach them.
You all have helped mold me into the best version
of myself to date.*

# INTRODUCTION

This book is a summation of the many important and critical concepts I have discovered, uncovered, or observed first hand. Over the past twenty years, I have been a practicing financial planner for those fifty years of age and older. I have been helping pre- and post-retirees preserve and grow assets, and derive consistent income for their lifetimes.

The challenges facing both financial advisors and investor-retirees are not exactly in short supply. For advisors, the challenges are reaching high levels of competence in the field as well as adapting to sudden changes. An even greater challenge for advisors is to effectively communicate fairly complex planning concepts, as well as financial product features, to every day people. I do not mean to imply that non-financial professionals are not smart enough to understand financial concepts. However, when someone does not specialize in a field as complex and comprehensive as financial planning, the learning curve can be enormous and very costly. While going it alone can be tempting, mistakes will be made and there will be a price for those mistakes. Prudent people do not want to experiment with their nest egg. Because there is so much deception and untruth in the financial media and the industry itself, I have felt compelled to blow the whistle on them. Yes, I have the audacity to think we can save the world one investor at a time with the truth made simple. Yes, it is time to break all of these deceptions down to the "skinny" and then, you the reader, can make up your own mind as to what you would like to do to make the most of your money and your future.

I have always been a champion for the investor. As I have been reviewing and analyzing portfolios for two decades, I have seen certain repetitive patterns of behavior as well as bizarre product recommendations clearly not in a client's best interest. I have also cringed at the mere sight of despicable shysters like Bernie Madoff or the Ohio-based crook, Frank Gruttadoria. The good news for most people is if we catch problems early, we can rectify them, and even reduce or undo the damage completely. The bad news for a small percentage of people, even after clear third-party evidence, is that they still remain frozen in the default position. I liken this mindset to the idea that the devil you know is better than the devil you don't.

**"The Skinny On How To Have A Fat Retirement"** is a collection of facts that will dispel many of the common myths and misconceptions people have about money and how they make financial decisions. The myths and misconceptions explained in this book stem from illogical ideas and the many falsehoods and smokescreens perpetuated by both the media as well as the financial industry itself. The media is your enemy. Information overload and irresponsible advice flood the airwaves. A complete lack of accountability is the unfortunate trend of the current financial news media.

In order for readers to improve their financial decision making, this book's intention is to appeal to your logical and rational side. Far too often, crucial and critical financial facts are either missed or misunderstood by investors. Part of the reason for this is because people often make financial decisions based on emotions such as fear, greed, or they are just simply misled by improper financial advice. These myths and misconceptions cost people countless dollars over their investing lifetime. Many times, the root of the problem does not lie in the actual management of most investments *per se*. But they stem from the fees, charges, costs, and improper tax planning of the financial advice given. This book will take the reader step-by-step through the discovery process and will show exactly how to assess the truth of where you are now with your retirement planning. More importantly, my hope is that it will help the reader make better financial decisions going forward.

We will discover how to recognize and reduce many of the unnecessary fees, costs, and taxes that are causing your retirement dollars to be falling through the cracks in your portfolio and retirement plan. Instead of just holding on to money with no real plan or design, the reader will finally be able to wrap their arms around their money. A clear plan based on facts should provide for you and your spouse's financial security for as long as you both live. Even if you utilize the help of an ethical and qualified financial professional in planning and implementing your retirement plan, you owe it to yourself, your partner, and your family to make the best financial decisions possible. My intent is to empower the reader to make financial decisions based on facts, not myths and misconceptions.

**"The Skinny on How to Have a Fat Retirement"** is intended to be a substantive and concise primer to expose the real "money snatchers." What are the money snatchers? They are the nameless and faceless things that rob you of your wealth. The money snatchers come in the form of high and hidden costs and fees. These costs are often not fully disclosed to clients with equal enthusiasm as they purport potential returns or benefits. The money snatchers are often less noticeable during bull market runs, such as the last twenty-year bull market up to the crash of 2008. One significant and undeniable result of the Great Recession is that people have grown more cognizant of costs and risks that *can* and *do* rob them of much of their savings. Indeed people are now more aware of the concept of risk and want to know how much risk they are really taking. Risk downside is greatly magnified for those over 50 years of age. Many have come to realize that the inevitable great drawdowns from market corrections can be recovered only so many times during one's lifetime.

My hope for all readers is an awakened and increased awareness of the falsehoods perpetuated by the financial services industry.

Do not blindly keep drinking the Kool-Aid of Wall Street Media. I urge all readers to take back control of their money by virtue of uncovering the truth.

Everyone is in business to make a living. Most people would agree with that. Some of us wish to act as stewards of the financial services industry as well as being successful professionals. From my personal experience of reviewing hundreds of portfolios, I can honestly say at least 80% of people are paying 1 to 3% _more_ each year than is necessary on their investments. This has a negative cumulative effect, which becomes staggering over time. Additionally, they receive insufficient tax advice that can be very damaging, resulting in continuous erosion of their savings.

In the following chapters, I will take you through a journey and a process that has been developed with _real_ people in the _real_ world. The process has been equally effective with people with investable assets from $250,000 to $25,000,000. One thing we all know about life is that change is a constant. The planning process is a living, breathing thing and should be viewed as an evolving process as times change and your lives change.

Please enjoy the following chapters with a refreshing "no holds barred" description of what really goes on between Wall Street and investors.

One more thought... In certain chapters it was unavoidable to get a bit complicated. You see, the book will be read by both the general public as well as the financial profession. I must be complete in my explanations and must be ready to defend my positions when challenged.

I thank you in advance for investing your valuable time to educate yourself and giving me the honor of sharing with you the many truths I have discovered the hard way. These facts have come from years of practice through bull markets, terrorist attacks, small recessions, prolonged Presidential elections, the

Great Recession, and the upcoming fiscal policy cliff our country is facing today.

# CHAPTER 1

# THE SKINNY ON THE 5-QUESTIONS YOU SHOULD ASK ANY ADVISOR *AND* THE 3-STEP PROCESS

*What is wanted is not the will to believe, but the will to find out, which is the exact opposite.* ~ Bertrand Russell

Understandably, many people want to have a certain amount of their nest egg kept very safe, while others want to have a specific income plan, and still others want a part or all of their money to beat inflation. Throughout this book I will cover these concerns and will also identify the many myths, misconceptions, hearsay, and confusion, which prevents people from obtaining or achieving their optimal financial potential.

My overall goal is to help people make better financial decisions. In light of that objective, I want to impart to you some of what I have developed over the last twenty years, so you can all make better decisions going forward. But, first you need to determine exactly how you make financial decisions. Unfortunately, many people make financial decisions based upon emotions and not on facts. As we all probably know, financial decisions based on emotion can be very damaging as well as costly. Financial decisions based unknowingly on myths, result in immediate or future losses of money and financial problems, that may or may not be correctable.

## What do you ask an advisor if you don't know what you don't know?

What is even more significant is that people often don't even know what questions to ask an advisor when making important financial decisions. I'm going to provide the five questions you should ask every financial advisor. You will be able to use this as your filter. If you don't get satisfactory answers to those five questions, then you most likely need to move on to another financial advisor.

## THE FIVE QUESTIONS YOU SHOULD ASK ANY FINANCIAL ADVISOR

**Questions One: Have you adequately reviewed my personal financial situation to make sure this recommendation is in my best interest?**

This sounds simple. But, it will take at least two meetings to gather the necessary information to develop an appropriate analysis of your current situation. If the financial advisor has not taken time to ask you probing questions about your current financial situation before you are offered a financial plan, you will know he may not be very thorough. Unfortunately, sometimes in this business, clients are given recommendations before any upfront data gathering takes place. This occurs more with product salesman than actual advisors. At other times, only a cursory gathering of information takes place making it impossible to develop a comprehensive financial plan. This step is so important that the Certified Financial Planner Board of Standards recommends the first step in the financial planning process is to gather information and analyze the data for the client well before any recommendations are made.

## Question Two: How will your plan affect my tax return each year and what future tax issues may concern me?

Many advisors give advice from a pure accumulation and an investment standpoint, but they fail to take into consideration what will be the annual or future tax erosion of that investment. Many people fear market risk and are alarmed at the very thought of losing money in the market. However, a financial strategy that is implemented with unknown tax results can actually become a bigger collective loss than one bad year in the market. That's why you will see later in this chapter, when we discuss "The Three-Step Review," that smart financial planning starts with looking at your tax return and identifying things such as "phantom income tax". There are many pitfalls created from inefficient tax investments and it takes a well-trained and experienced financial advisor to prevent this. A good advisor can help you implement strategies that will benefit you most in the short as well as the long term. Often people will focus on the wrong things and ignore the tax implications, but it is vitally important to evaluate both. I cannot over-emphasize the magnitude of this point. If your financial advisor has not even looked at your tax return, you need to ask, "Why?" Depending on the answer, you will likely need to find another advisor.

## Question Three: How will your plan affect my income as well as my liquidity needs in the future?

Unfortunately, many plans or products are "sold" to people, but they fail to take into consideration things such as liquid emergency funds. These are funds the client should keep off to the side and separate from their investment and income plans. Once again, if you don't get an adequate answer, you will want to consider moving to another advisor. However, many seniors greatly overestimate the amounts needed for emergencies and they get very little return on that money for many years, which add up to a lot of lost opportunity costs.

## Question Four: How does your plan match up with my risk comfort level?

Financial advisors have always asked this question regarding risk. Yet, historically many investors have often taken more risk than they were able to accept when the downside occurs. One of the good things that have come out of the "Great Recession" of 2008, is people are now seriously looking at the consequences of risk. Prior to 2008, people were getting intoxicated with the potential rates of return on their investments, which were virtually unsustainable. Investors today have actually seen loss first-hand and recently in their own accounts as well as in the accounts of people that were just about to retire. They see how those losses drastically and permanently affect their ability to obtain the highest income going forward. Risk assessment is essential to prudent financial planning and that is why it is part of the upcoming "Three-step Process." People are now willing to listen to the topic of risk. Those that listened to me before 2008 have retained far more than those that did not.

## Question Five: How will your plan affect the transition of my estate to my heirs?

This question is about legacy. The first objective for a financial advisor should be to make sure their client will not outlive their money and that they never have to ask their children for money or have to move in with their children. Many people think that the greatest gift you can give your children and yourself is to never *have* to live with them if you do not want. Legacy is another very important component of sound financial planning. You should know what will happen at various stages of your financial plan, and especially when you come to the point of transferring your assets. Unfortunately, some salespeople can be a little sloppy when it comes to designating beneficiaries. Sometimes they're ready to move on to their next appointment or the next client and they don't take the time to clearly identify your beneficiaries. Will your estate plan go through probate or will it bypass probate? How will this affect my heirs? Your financial advisor should be able to answer these questions very easily. You will want to make sure that the value of your estate will go to your designated beneficiaries and not to the government or probate lawyers.

So, there you have it; the five critical questions you should ask any financial advisor. Just these five questions alone, have now made you more empowered than 90% of your peers. You should use these queries to empower yourself when dealing with your current advisor or future advisors. After all, the main purpose of this book is to help people regain ownership of their money.

## THE 3-STEP REVIEW PROCESS

I would like to describe the Three-Step Review process and how the "five questions" get answered as a natural course of this process. This logical and proven process incorporates the "Five Questions" and much more. It helps to ensure the five questions are answered to your satisfaction. If the above questions have not been asked, or you are unsure if they have been answered rationally, then further review is warranted. Any financial recommendation should be explainable with a crayon and understandable by a child. If not, do not move forward. The Three-Step Review process will give you inroads to the truth, so you can rest assured your best interests remain at the core of your financial plan.

## THREE STEPS TO DISCOVERY

### Step One: A Complete Past and Look-Forward Tax Review Analysis

The first step of the three-step review process is a complete past and look-forward review. This step begins with analyzing your tax return to identify things like phantom income tax (which will be described in detail in the next chapter) or unnecessary annual taxation on assets. A qualified advisor can also scrutinize incorrect uses of tax deferral strategies, as well as uncovering missed opportunities for offsetting gains and losses. This could be as simple as selling a losing stock to offset capital gains on a mutual fund. This is what I call "finding the money in your couch."

## Step Two: Perform an Income Analysis

The second step of the review process is to do a complete income analysis. There are non-asset-based incomes such as Social Security and Pensions. There are also asset-based incomes or potential future incomes. There are basically three kinds of retirees in today's financial market: Retirees that need an income plan today and need to harvest their money now; retirees that need a little bit of money down the road to keep up with inflation or to replace a pension that is lost or reduced when one spouse dies; and retirees who are so fortunate that they never need an income plan at all. Some people don't know their future income needs, and that is why the income planning process is so important: To meet immediate or future income needs. However, this initial step is designed to make sure you are using your income sources properly and in the most tax efficient way, that you have adequate income to meet your future needs and that you have a plan to offset the ever-increasing cost of inflation.

## Step Three: Analyzing Your Investment Costs and Risk Exposure

The third step in the review process is a combination of looking at your investment cost fees as well as your investment risk exposure. It is imperative that your risk exposure is one in which you are comfortable and is in line with what you want. Research shows that people make poor decisions, receive low rates of return, and incur losses because they incur more risk than they realize. I will elaborate more on this subject in the "risk" chapter.

Investment costs should be analyzed by a third-party such as Morningstar and quantified line-by-line for you with a complete description of each cost.

The above Three-Step Review process is a logical and stepwise process that can be used before making any financial decision.

For example, if you're contemplating selling a piece of real estate or a highly-appreciated business, the first step of the review is to look at your tax return to determine what the tax ramifications will be when you sell. Is it an income property or principal residence? Other things associated may be exposed or a problem may be compounded by the sale of the property and this process will enable you to prepare for the loss or implement the proper strategy to lower or eliminate the consequential tax. To continue with the property sale example, the second step would be to do an income analysis to determine if you are using income sources correctly.

What kind of income will you be able to derive from the money you get from the property? Or, if it's an income investment property, can you go without that source of additional revenue? Then, during the risk analysis you would look at making sure that you get your financial house in order before you sell the property. You would need to determine if the decision to sell is right for you and if you will be able to make the transition in life with peace of mind.

You shouldn't rush the financial planning process. When you find the right financial advisor, take whatever time is necessary, ask the five questions and be sure to do a thorough look-forward review and analysis. Take control of your finances by following the process I have outlined, and the chapters of this book. It is time people reclaim ownership of their retirement. The only way to accomplish that is by seeing through all of the falsehoods and misinformation from the financial industry. Your future depends on it.

# CHAPTER 2

# THE SKINNY ON PHANTOM INCOME TAX

*The hardest thing in the world to understand is the income tax.*
~ Albert Einstein

Before explaining the Phantom Income Tax, it will be helpful to have a full understanding of **mutual funds**. Many people are familiar with the term, "mutual fund," but not everyone understands how mutual funds work. Mutual funds were created by the Investment Company Act of 1940 and are regulated by the Securities and Exchange Commission (SEC). As you may know, a stock is an individual share of ownership in a company. A mutual fund is made up of a pool of funds from many investors for the purpose of investing in securities such as stocks, bonds, money market instruments, and similar assets. Each shareholder participates proportionally in the gain or loss of the fund. When you put your money in a mutual fund, instead of buying individual stocks or bonds, you put it with an investment company. The most commonly known investment companies include Fidelity, Vanguard, and Putnam. The investment company will manage the account at their will within the stated objectives of the funds charter in the prospectus.

## WHAT IS PHANTOM INCOME TAX?

I have found it to be interesting and eye opening to ask people attending my workshops and seminars if they have ever heard of Phantom Income Tax. Rarely do I ever see a hand go up. If someone does raise their hand, they are usually my client and have learned about this hidden tax from our team.

Now, if I ask if there's anyone in the room that had one of their funds go down in value in a year or more, but still received a capital gains tax bill in the form of a 1099 from the mutual fund company, there are usually two or three hands that go up indicating they have experienced that scenario. What they don't realize is that the 1099 they received from the fund is Phantom Income Tax. This is tax due on money you never had to spend in the first place. This is the equivalent of getting kicked in the head after someone runs you over with their car.

Take a moment to let this sink in: **Their mutual fund lost money for the year, yet they were taxed on gains inside it; gains they never had a chance to use or spend at all. Instead they have to write a check to the IRS after a year of flat or down performance.**

Let me explain how this happens. Mutual funds do not pay federal income taxes on the funds bought and sold within the fund. Gains on non-IRA mutual funds are passed on to the shareholders, this occurs often when your account is flat or down on the year. Phantom Income Tax occurs when more winners than losers are realized (made real and taxable), in a year by the fund.

Allow me to elaborate. For example, individual stocks within a mutual fund will fluctuate daily. Some days they will be up in price and some days they will be down. But, they are not fated to be "winners" or "losers" until they are sold. That is when a "realized gain" or a "realized loss" takes place. It is very possible for a fund manager to sell off stock for a gain, but still have the mutual fund lose money over the course of a year. If a portion of the mutual fund is sold for a gain, the investor then becomes responsible for the taxation on that capital gain, even if the value on your statement is less than it was at the beginning of the year.

Until the fund manager actually sells the losers, they cannot be used to offset the winners that were "realized" within the fund. So, the difference is not just how many winners and losers there are over a year, but how many winners and losers have been "realized" or sold. Keep in mind, the fund manager's job is to maximize the portfolio for maximum return and they are going to try to show more winners than losers. The key here is having a clear understanding of "realized" gains and losses versus "un-realized" gains and losses. Again, realized gains or losses occur when the stock is sold by the fund. It can lose money inside the portfolio, but the realization of that loss or gain is not "real" until it is sold. So, once again, the value of a mutual fund can be down, but it will only be realized when it is sold. It's when you have more realized gains than realized losses in a year that Phantom Income taxes are triggered.

## REAL LIFE EXAMPLE

I had a couple come to me with this very problem. They had $350,000 invested in a portfolio of various mutual funds and the account lost about $90,000 in one year. That was approximately a 27% loss, but they still had a capital gain of about $1,500 (paid $225 in taxes) at the end of the year. They were victims of Phantom Income Tax. It's very likely someone reading this book has had something very similar happen to them. In this case, the fund had gone up a lot in the first half of the year, and then, it flattened during the second half of the year. The mutual fund manager sold the winners because he wanted to realize wins. Remember, the mutual fund manager's objective is to make money for the fund. His objective is not to do *your* tax planning. They are focused on keeping their job by getting the highest returns possible. They are under immense pressure to produce winners. This is not a criticism of fund managers. It is simply an explanation of how mutual funds and Phantom Income tax works, and how it affects your bottom line

## How does this affect you?

When you are taxed on a realized gain, this becomes an involuntary assessed taxation on a gain that you never even had in your hand to use. In other words, you never had the money to spend, but you still had to pay tax on it. This is the Phantom Income Tax you want to avoid.

## How often does Phantom Income Tax happen?

It happens three to four years out of every ten. 2013 is a classic scenario of a calendar year that triggers Phantom Income Tax. You often have a strong market in the first four to six months of the calendar year. Then it's either flat or down for the remainder of the year. This pattern is just one of many patterns that occur repeatedly over time. It's the nature of the beast, which is the market.

## Why does the Phantom Income Tax happen with mutual funds and not stocks or ETF's?

While it is possible, Phantom Income Tax does not frequently happen in Exchange Traded Funds or ETF's. It happens in mutual funds more often due to the regulatory construct of active mutual funds versus the tax treatment of stocks or ETF gains. It's really that simple. Phantom income tax is like keeping your shower on 24 hours a day when it's used for only less than one hour. Waste is waste.

## How can you reduce or eliminate Phantom Income Tax?

If you own mutual funds solely, you cannot control it. The fund is actually in control of your money from a tax standpoint. However, if you have other assets, you can use them to offset some Phantom Income Tax by taking realized losses on some of your other investments.

You can also entirely eliminate Phantom Income Tax by substituting mutual funds with stocks or ETF's. By doing this, you can exercise more control over when YOU realize capital gains and you're not at the random and unpredictable mercy of the investment company. In other words, YOU are in control of how and when you are taxed. Not somebody else.

## Why aren't you told about Phantom Income Tax when you purchased mutual funds?

There are actually a couple of reasons. First, there is a lack of transparency intrinsic in the very minimal regulations of these funds. Really, it's a tax consequence that comes from what it is. Mutual funds are not required to report Phantom Income Tax potential.

Second, a commissioned salesperson is not required to tell about the potential of a Phantom Income Tax. In fact, many of them are not even aware of Phantom Income Tax. A lack of tax knowledge by the advisor alone is a plausible reason they never bring it to the attention of an investor.

Phantom income tax is not anything illegal or unethical. However, it is kicking you and your investments while they are down. It's not the most attractive feature of a mutual fund.

## What should your financial advisor do if you have mutual funds invested in a non-IRA?

As a financial advisor, the first thing I would do is look at your tax return. That's part of the three-step review discussed in the previous chapter. The standard for sound tax planning is to first identify it, then quantify it, and rectify it. By reviewing your tax return we can see the exact source of any gain because it will be listed in an itemized section of the tax return. Unfortunately, anything that has already happened is history and cannot be reversed. However, your advisor can make recommendations to help you avoid Phantom Income Tax in the future. A good advisor will always look at things going forward to determine how to prevent these types of unintended consequences.

## What alternative investments can I use to avoid the Phantom Income Tax?

Personally, I believe ETF's are a logical answer to the Phantom Income Tax issue faced by mutual fund investors. I have found that I help clients accomplish their financial objectives with less taxation, no Phantom Income Tax, and less net expenses by using Exchange Traded Funds. You don't have to have the risk of individual stock. An ETF is only one piece of a diversified portfolio that has possibly hundreds of stocks inside it, so you don't have the intrinsic risk that you do with individual stocks. ETF's are more tax efficient and if they are used in a proper design you can achieve a very respectable return on a tax favored basis with minimal cost.

## How can I find out if a mutual fund is vulnerable to the Phantom Income Tax?

If you want to do your own research, you can find resources that will give you information about particular funds that will give you a clue about their tendencies toward a Phantom Income Tax. One of the best resources is the MorningStar Report. MorningStar is an independent rating service for mutual funds, stocks and exchange-traded funds. In that report you would look at the turnover statistics for the mutual fund. The level of turnover will be the "canary in the coalmine" when sniffing for Phantom Income Tax potential. If the turnover percentage is over 50% per year, you are beginning to get into the likely "Phantom Income Tax" zone. Many funds have 80%, 150%, and even much higher. In global funds, the price spread is greater than domestic funds and 100% turnover could cost you an additional 3% per year or more.

Turnover is when a mutual fund manager at an investment company buys and sells his whole portfolio in a twelve month period. In other words, if you look at a MorningStar report and you see that turnover is at 100% or higher, which is fairly common, that means that manager bought and sold every single position that he started with in the course of the year. If it's

300%, it means the fund manager has bought and sold every single position that he started with 3 times in the course of a year. Along with certain market trends, higher turnover can trigger a lot of Phantom Income Tax. Conversely, any fund with less than a 10% turnover rate would generate a very minimal Phantom Income Tax.

### Is Phantom Income Tax something that a tax preparer or CPA should alert you to?

Accountants and tax preparers understand the concept of Phantom Income Tax and can explain it. However, it is unlikely they will take the time to offer any advice regarding how to eliminate it. When a tax preparer has hundreds or even thousands of tax returns running through their office in any given year, they have a very limited amount of time they can spare to offer advice for future planning for any individual. They are looking at your tax return more as a historian. There are a number of great tax preparers and CPAs that do forward tax planning, but the majority of them typically do not have the time because their time is consumed with getting large volumes of returns prepared. Tax preparers have a very difficult job, because the IRS code is constantly changing and highly complex.

## FINAL THOUGHTS ON THE PHANTOM INCOME TAX

Phantom Income Tax can be a cause of thousands of dollars falling through the cracks in your tax planning. When you consider being concerned about market losses and the volatility of the market, Phantom Income Tax happens in addition to those things. It is just another financial erosion to your investments. The good news is it is something you can actually take control of by implementing a fairly simple strategy of alternative investments that will still enable you to achieve your financial objectives, without unwanted and untimely taxation.

# CHAPTER 3

# THE SKINNY ON VOLUNTARY ANNUAL TAXATION OF YOUR ASSETS

*The avoidance of taxes is the only intellectual pursuit that carries any reward.* ~ John Maynard Keynes

For the purposes of this chapter, I would like you to take a 30,000-foot view of all of your assets. For the next few minutes as you read this chapter, forget about all the performance-related features of your investments and look at the entire pool of your money as one lump sum. For this exercise, think about combining all of your investments...your savings, trusts, individuals, IRA's, joint accounts...only temporarily, to focus on the following concept.

Now that you have lumped all of your assets together in your mind, I would like you to then split them into two sub-divisions of currently taxable and not currently taxable. That is, IRA's and non-IRA's.

As you may already know, IRA's are tax-deferred until money is withdrawn. They are taxable at the highest ordinary income rates for an individual or couple. Non-IRA's are not tax-deferred, but can be positioned into tax-deferred status. However, non-IRA's are taxed only on the gain *above* your principal. Non-IRA's are things like joint accounts, revocable living trust accounts, individual accounts, TOD's, and POD's.

Again, for the sake of the exercise in this chapter, think of all your money in terms of the tax qualities of each of the two types of taxable sets (100% taxable IRA vs. Taxable only on the gain Non-IRA's). Do this in your mind so you can follow the line of thinking of this concept.

Let's first look at one point. Most advisors and self-investors think about the returns, costs, risks, and all of the other prudent things one should consider when making an investment. Those things are *crucial* and *critical* points. However, before an advisor gives you a recommendation, they, and you, need to fully understand the investment's current tax treatment as well as its later tax treatment, and even how is it taxed when you die. Unfortunately, tax consequence is a point many people miss and it can have a significant impact on your assets.

You will recall that in the previous chapter we covered and recognized Phantom Income Tax (PIT) in Non-IRA accounts as a real cost that can greatly reduce your net returns on an annual basis. If you are still unclear about Phantom Income Tax, I suggest you stop here and re-read the previous chapter. You see, before you make any investment, you should first look at it in an accurate tax context. Unfortunately, many advisors put the cart before the horse when making investment recommendations that can set the investor up for substantial financial losses.

Now that you have, in your mind, divided all of your assets into IRA's and non-IRA's, let's take this a step further and look at these concepts in three parts.

## TAX POCKET NUMBER 1

In Tax Pocket Number 1 you should only designate current income-generating assets that you need to live on and are using to meet your current living expenses. This could be non-IRA money. It could be money that you use as an income stream from an IRA, but once you take it out of the IRA it becomes non-IRA money. This amount will vary from person-to-person and from household-to-household depending on the chosen lifestyle and level of monthly expenses.

As you know, if you are receiving income from an asset, the IRS requires you to pay tax on it by April 15th of the year following the year it was received. For the purposes of this chapter, we will assume there are no other sophisticated tax reduction strategies being used to offset any taxable income.

So once again, if you are receiving income in this calendar year, you will be subject to current income tax. Most people do not argue this point. If you are taking income this year, it is only appropriate that you should pay current taxes.

Unfortunately, many, many investors are paying tax on much more than what they are using for living expenses. Because they have more in Tax Pocket Number 1 than just their living expense money. They are receiving income, interest, and or dividends on a "tax-disadvantaged" basis (highest ordinary income brackets) when they are not using that money to live on in the current year. What is the result? The result is an annual depletion of your funds by repetitive runaway taxes on the income (income you currently aren't using) from assets. Consequently, you have lost the purchasing power of the money lost each year and the future opportunity the lost money would bring. Think about it.

Line 8a on the IRS 1040 tax return will show the tax-exposed income from interest and ordinary dividends. This income is added to your other earned and investment income for the year and is consequently reduced by current taxation, year after year, after year. This is just another one of the ways money falls through the cracks for people time and time again. At the end of this chapter I will show you the remedies on how to plug this hole in your financial boat.

In summary, you should only have money in Tax Pocket Number 1 if you are living on the income from those assets in the current year.

## TAX POCKET NUMBER 2

Assets in Tax Pocket Number 2 should be reserved for income you MAY need on a sporadic basis or you MAY need to generate additional income at some indefinite time in the future. This pocket is for unscheduled or unplanned lumps. Pocket Number 2 is best utilized as an intermediate "war chest" to be used for income to replace pensions or Social Security Income lost from the death of a spouse. This bucket could also be used for additional income to supplement other income streams, such as social security or pensions, for greater buying power. In other words, when inflation starts to noticeably give you less mileage per dollar than it used to, you would use income from the assets in Tax Pocket Number 2, as you need it. But, until you DO need it, it should not be subject to annual taxation like funds in Tax Pocket Number 1.

Let me give you an analogy. If you came to my house for dinner one evening, and as we were dining, you heard the shower running upstairs. At that point you may ask, "Is someone upstairs taking a shower?" I would respond, "No. I leave the shower on just in case I may want to take a shower later this evening." You would think I was crazy, and you would be right. You would think I was insane to waste water in such a manner, instead of just turning it on and off only when needed.

If you think wasting water is foolish, then what do you think about people who pay voluntary annual taxation on money they are not currently using? There is absolutely no difference. Waste is waste.

Here is another example of how ludicrous waste can be. Paying unnecessary taxes on unneeded current income is like leaving all of the lights on in your house at all times, when you and your spouse are sitting and reading in the den. You leave the lights on in every room because you MAY need to walk into one of those rooms at sometime during the evening. You would say, "That's a ridiculous waste of electricity." Again, you would be absolutely correct. So, you can see how subjecting money you are not currently utilizing to annual taxation... is no less ridiculous than the shower or lighting example. Yet, that's what many people do year after year.

The bottom line is this: If you aren't using the money, don't put it in investment vehicles where it will be subject to your highest current tax rates.

## TAX POCKET NUMBER 3

This tax pocket is the last bastion of funds for an individual or couple. In Tax Pocket Number 3, you should put the money you will probably never even touch in your lifetime. This is money that will likely be designated for your heirs or charity. This is typically legacy money and most certainly should not be subject to current taxation.

Things in this bucket may be assets such as Roth IRA's, Traditional IRA's, Life Insurance, and annuities with a lot of tax-deferred buildup.

### How do you know if you have the correct assets in the right pockets?

Your tax return will tell you if you have the correct assets in the right bucket. If you don't know how to obtain this information from your tax return, find a qualified person that can help you.

As stated in chapter one, the five questions to ask any financial salesperson involves these very tax issues. The 3-Step Review process uncovers any money falling through the cracks that will be revealed in your tax return, as well as investment costs and risk level.

## How do I stop these tax leaks?

I promised earlier in this chapter to provide you with some examples of how to stop these tax leaks from occurring in income producing assets you are not currently using. Here are five of the many solutions:

1. As I mentioned in the previous chapter, one of the solutions to stop Phantom Income Tax is to use Exchange Traded Funds or stocks instead of mutual funds in non-IRA accounts. ETF's have negligible turnover, thus no PIT. ETF's can also receive qualified dividend treatment (lower capital gains rates).

2. Have your tax-exposed funds in a growth portfolio that does not pay dividends. However, you should only use stocks, ETF's, or structured market portfolios to accomplish this. You should NOT use active mutual funds, or you will find yourself driving around the same tax "cul de sac" I have been describing.

3. You can shelter money in Tax Pocket Number 2 in a tax-deferred annuity. If you need unscheduled withdrawals they are available. Or, if you need to add a permanent income source at some future point, annuities can be a great resource for that as well. However, I would strongly caution you to avoid Variable Annuities, due to their heavy and often under-disclosed fees, charges and other costs.

4. You can use a cash-heavy, low death benefit, life insurance policy. From these accounts you can pull out tax-free money up to what you have funded it with. This is a very good tax-favored vehicle to use.

5. If you are wealthy, or somewhat wealthy, you can donate a highly appreciated business or property, receive tax-free income from a charitable trust, avoid the capital gain on the appreciated asset, and produce tax-free income to your heirs. This is accomplished through charitable remainder

trust planning with a wealth replacement trust. To establish this kind of trust planning, only work with advisors that are very qualified in this area. This is a very specialized area and must be done correctly. Not only do you need a financial advisor, you also need an attorney, a trust entity, and a CPA. But, it's worth it.

## SOME CONCLUDING THOUGHTS ON RUNAWAY TAXATION

I hope it has become apparent as to why I wanted you to only think of your assets in terms of taxable and tax-deferred assets. You will want to make sure you are paying taxes only on the money you are using to fund your current lifestyle. <u>More importantly, you should know the difference between the performance of an asset and the taxable treatment of an asset.</u> They are each very distinct and critical for financial success or failure.

At this point, some of you may still be confused. Don't feel bad. The Internal Revenue Code is very complicated, and without training or the help of a qualified investment advisor or tax advisor, it is easy to become confused and at a loss for direction.

At a minimum, the take-away from this chapter and the "Three Tax Pockets" concept should be that you have choices with how you can structure your investments, without giving up any investment advantage, to only generate "currently taxable" income on money you currently use to live. The other assets can and should be tax-sheltered until you need to access those for an unscheduled or unexpected event. You can also draw on any money you have to supplement your current income. Armed with this knowledge, you are now more empowered to have more control over how and when you generate taxable income so you can keep more of your money.

So far we have covered the questions that should be asked, the three-step review process, Phantom Income tax, and runaway annual taxation from non-IRA investments.

In the next chapter, we will discover how investment fees, costs, and charges are often the biggest culprits causing your money to fall through the cracks.

# CHAPTER 4

# THE SKINNY ON MUTUAL FUND AND VARIABLE ANNUITY COSTS, FEES, CHARGES, AND TURNOVER

*Expenses are what kill investor returns. The more expenses and people you have between you and your money, the less you keep.* ~ Warren Buffet

## MUTUAL FUNDS

Before discussing the costs, fees, and charges inside mutual funds and variable annuities, let's first look at the big picture. Many people get mesmerized watching and following the movements of the Dow Index or the S&P 500 Index. In this chapter I want to dispel yet another myth.

Myth: Often people think, after staring at the Dow Jones Industrial Average, that their portfolio should be doing the same as the Dow Industrial Average.

I have observed this phenomenon, and I can assure you it is a fallacy and a myth. There are a couple of reasons why most investments do not mirror the price movements of the Dow, and why it is only intuitive logic at work.

41

First, indexes do not take into consideration timing issues when building a portfolio. For indexes, there is no "getting in" and "getting out" of the market. Secondly, the indexes do not have costs associated with them. Costs are like pin holes in a balloon. They have the potential to deflate your financial balloon significantly.

A recent Dalbar study[1] vividly illustrates this reality. The study showed that the average return for investors for the last 20 years is only 3.6%. If we look at the last 10 years, it's less than negative one-half of one percent or (-0.50). There are two primary reasons for this outcome. Remember, indices are benchmarks, but there is no reason you should presume your money will follow the indices or even mirror the indices. The first reason for the dismal investor returns revealed in the Dalbar study, is investors often will get into an investment at the very worst time (new market highs) and also leave an investment at the very worst time (market lows). There are various reasons for this, but it happens. The second reason is that investors are not cognizant of the **TRUE** costs assessed on their capital (what their investments really cost in total). That's what I've been preaching for the past twenty years and that's what this chapter is about.

Before anyone ever goes into an investment, the first thing they should do is look at a MorningStar report on the fund or stock they are considering. Many financial professionals will print a report for you for free. If someone is presenting a mutual fund to you, they should show you a MorningStar report. We can all agree that a typical mutual fund prospectus is very long and wordy, and investors do not find them helpful. If for some reason they don't, I encourage you to ask the advisor for a third-party report.

There are four specific places on the report that should catch your attention. First, look at the "front-end load" of the fund. Some funds don't have a front-end load, but many do. A front-end load is an immediate cost you will incur to initially invest in a fund and it is an immediate drain on your short-term potential

---

1    2011 QAIB Qualitative Analysis of Investor Behavior prepared by Dalbar, Inc.
     Research & Communications Division March 2011

gain. Loads of any kind put you in the hole on the very day you go into the market and drag on it long-term. For example, if the net asset value (NAV) of the fund is $100, your 5.75% load makes you buy-in at $105.75 dollars. This starts you off at a loss the very first day you purchase a fund. In other words, until the mutual fund's price goes up to $105.75, you are at a loss.

Secondly, you should also look at the 12b-1 fees. The 12b-1 fee is derived from the regulatory code that governs this fee. It is simply an annual marketing and advertising fee that is assessed to the fund holders of the fund. This expense is primarily so a fund can advertise and get *more* people to invest in the mutual fund. This fee is considered an operational expense and is generally between 0.25% and 1% or more annually.

## BY THE WAY...OWNERS OF MUTUAL FUNDS GET CAUGHT IN TWO TRAPS:

A. Most funds must stay 80% invested at all times. This means that when markets periodically dip or even crash, your funds are still sitting in the middle of the market pounding.

B. Fund holders that unknowingly hang on to their funds after massive cash outflows of redemptions in bad times. This means your share price goes down proportionately with more funds outflows.

Third, there is also a gross expense that you should uncover. These expenses are clearly stated. They range from 0.25% to 2%.

Fourth, usually located in the far right corner of the report, is a number called "turnover." The turnover number is shown as a percentage. As mentioned in the previous chapter, where I discussed Phantom Income Tax, a 100% turnover means the fund manager bought and sold 100% of the portfolio within a 12-month period. So, if you see 50%, it means that the fund manager turned over half of the portfolio. If you see 300%, it means he turned over the portfolio three times in one year. Why is this important? This is important because stocks have a spread between what they are bought and sold for. This spread, or difference, is where the market makers on the floor of the exchanges make their money. Turnover incurs this spread cost inside the fund. The spread in US domestic stocks is comparatively lower than global spreads. So 100% turnover in a fund that is primarily US invested can be 1.5% per year. A global fund with wide spreads can be as high as 5% per year in turnover. Also, US large company stocks have thinner spreads than domestic small cap stocks. Therefore small-cap funds have higher turnover costs than large-cap funds. Investors do not get a bill for turnover, so that is why it remains hidden until enlightened by the truth. Turnover costs are reflected in the form of a lack of return. So, you have to translate that cost based on the turnover rate and add that to the total cost of the fund. These turnover costs are NOT reflected in a mutual fund's public performance returns. Do not let yourself be fooled.

*In review:* To properly evaluate a fund, you must be cognizant of the front-end load, the 12b-1 fees, the gross expenses, and the expense due to the turnover rate. The total of that number will give you the true cost for that fund. Keep in mind that you don't get a bill for the turnover and it's consequences are not clearly stated in the prospectus. That's why the cost associated with the turnover rate gets by the public so easily and is often undetected. However, once a person knows what to look for, they usually don't allow that cost to get by them again. These fees are one of the biggest reasons why individual mutual funds will not mirror the indexes.

Once again, when a fund reports performance on the fund, they report the gross growth, not growth minus expenses or net returns. In my opinion, we need more regulation on mutual funds that will increase disclosure and transparency for the safety and benefit of the public. The investor should not have to translate the real costs associated with an investment. All the related expenses should be explained in writing so there is no question or even a hint of non-disclosure. My personal opinion is that the fund should be required to translate the turnover rate into actual stated costs and clearly state it on the MorningStar report along-side the 12b-1 fees and operating expenses. Incidentally, a lack of fee disclosure is one of the biggest reasons people leave their current advisor.

## VARIABLE ANNUITIES
## (NOT FIXED OR INDEXED ANNUITIES)

The same expenses we find in mutual funds are also found in variable annuities. But, there is even more to consider when evaluating a variable annuity. There are two primary categories of annuities. Fixed annuities (including indexed annuities) are the first category and variable annuities are the second catego-ry. In a way, "variable annuity" gives the term "annuity" a bad name. When you think about it, a variable annuity is just the op-posite of the fixed annuity. The first annuity concept originated as a safe tax-deferred investment vehicle or one that paid a pen-sion for life. The variable annuity stripped the safety feature out of the traditional annuity by tieing the returns of the annuity to the market and is not protected from it.

To properly evaluate a variable annuity, you must take the four mutual fund evaluation components we just discussed and add yet another expense. Variable Annuities have a "mortality and expense fee" (M&E) of typically around 1.25% in addition to all the other fees we discussed associated with mutual funds. What does the M&E fee do? It pays a higher value when you die. It's like buying the most expensive insurance policy avail-able. For example, if your variable annuity has a death benefit of $105,000, and your surrender value is $100,000 (which your family would get anyway upon your death) the variable annuity owner is paying over 1% per year, each and every year, on the entire account for only $5,000 more of a death benefit than is available anyway. M&E costs are the most expensive life insur-ance in the world. A variable annuity used for an IRA is even more improper. Think about it. All of these fees and life insur-ance costs on an IRA? Who needs that? It's not illegal, but it is inappropriate.

Sadly, in the twenty years I've been a financial advisor, I've never had anyone come to my office with a variable annuity who was actually told the complete truth about the associated expenses when they purchased it. Many were told it was some sort of "market protection," but that's not really true. Your heart has to stop for that "market protection" to become effective. It is basically buying a very expensive life insurance policy on the little bit of gain you may derive from your variable annuity.

Again, one of the worst scenarios is when someone has an IRA inside a variable annuity. They are a paying insurance costs on a retirement account. This doesn't make sense because you're going to see an additional 3% to 4% year after year, being paid in expenses each and every year for the variable annuity.

In summary and to restate: The variable annuity has a tax deferral benefit just like a fixed annuity. However, it's really in the market. It has all the basic mutual fund costs associated with it plus the M&E fees.

The bottom line is this, if you want to be in the market, be in the market. But look at alternatives that are lean, liquid, and low in expenses. Using indexing or structured market funds have proven to outperform 80% to 90% of all active fund managers. Let me say that again. It's a fact that over 80% to 90% (depending on which study you look at), of active mutual fund managers, who are paid millions, cannot even beat the basic indexes. If they are not meeting or beating the market, and you also have the fees and expenses we previously discussed, how productive will that mutual fund or variable annuity investment be for you?

If you want to be in the market, I will show you how to be in the market without incurring runaway costs, fees and turnover charges. These are things that usually are not explained to the public. When I go through initial discovery with a potential client, it is often the first time in their life they have seen the complete truth regarding the costs of their current investments. Usually, when they discover how much money they have been losing unnecessarily in their investments, they are open to considering an alternative that will be more productive. Unfortunately, they realize how much money has been taken from them in their previous investments that they will never be able to recover.

If you know these costs are taking place, and you choose to be involved with a particular investment product, then that is simply a choice you make. However, if you don't know about the expenses and costs associated with the investment product, then there's something ethically wrong with being sold that type of product. I've talked to hundreds of people over the past twenty years and, unfortunately, this is a common tale for investors.

In summary, mutual funds have a series of listed expenses. Variable annuities have 3-5% annual expenses. Some may be higher than others. But, you really don't know what the expenses are until you look at a report that will disclose all this information. I've explained turnover and how turnover can greatly impact your money and increase your expenses, but these expenses are not made transparent to you by a salesman. Because these things have not been disclosed to you directly, you're not being protected. I like to simply show people the truth and let them determine what is right for them. We also discussed variable annuities and the related expenses. They have even bigger expenses when you add the insurance costs.

These high expense variable annuities and mutual funds are not the only game in town. There are plenty of ways one can make much greater returns with less cost and more tax efficiency. That's what this book is all about, and I will offer some specific alternatives in chapter 8. If someone like Warren Buffett cares about how much his expenses are in his investments, then why should we treat our money any differently? I want to help people learn how to respect their money. What do I mean by that? People don't want to lose their money, but there's more demanded from you if you really want to respect your money.

Respecting your money means educating yourself regarding financial decisions you make. A good financial advisor can be a great teacher for those interested in learning. The fact that you are reading this book says you are someone that is interested in respecting their money and making wise investment decisions. Kudos to you.

# CHAPTER 5

# THE SKINNY ON DIVIDEND PAYING STOCKS AND DRIP'S

## DIVIDENDS CAN COME IN THE FORM OF CASH OR SHARES OF STOCK

Before discussing dividend paying stocks and DRIPs, it is important to define what and how "total return" of your investment is calculated. "Total return" is simply defined as the total amount of money a particular investment has yielded over a specific period of time from a combination of the dividends, if paid out, and then the net gain or loss on a stock's physical value. For example, if you earned a 2% cash or stock dividend and your stock went up 1%, your total return is 3%. The combination of these two factors, measured over a specific period of time, will give you the "total return" on your stock. A stock can yield a dividend, and yet still go down in price. This would result in a lower net total return. As you can see, there are always variables that will have an impact on your total return. This chapter will identify factors that will affect the total return on your investments.

Another term important to this chapter that needs to be defined is "blue chip stock." The term "blue chip" was derived from casinos and the game of poker where the blue chips are identified as the most valuable chips on the table. Blue chip stocks are stocks of large, well established, and financially sound companies that have operated for many years. A company that is considered blue chip typically has a market capitalization in the billions, is generally a market leader or among the top three companies in its sector, and is often a household name. While paying dividends is not absolutely necessary for a stock to be considered blue chip, most blue chips have a record of paying stable or rising dividends for years if not decades. They are traditionally thought to be a "safe" investment. The word "safe" is thrown around inappropriately about lots of things like gold. Blue chip stocks and gold for instance, are not likely to go down to zero, but they sure can fall below your principal or original investment at any time. I want the reader to never forget that a blue chip stock is still an equity-based investment and there is no equity-based investment that is safe or principal protected. Yet, blue chip companies are thought to be in excellent financial shape and firmly entrenched as a leader in their respective fields.

## DIVIDEND PAYING STOCKS

Growth companies do not typically pay dividends, because profits and retained earnings are plowed back into growth-oriented activities, as opposed to paying out some profits or retained earnings in the form of cash or stock dividends to the equity holders. The main characteristic of blue chip stocks is they generally pay dividends. Keep in mind, dividends are not required to be paid out by a company. But once a company starts paying dividends, any missed quarterly dividends would prove disastrous for a company's perceived value and stability. A company that stops or greatly reduces dividends from prior levels will get hammered in the stock market. Some companies have gotten away with lowering dividends such as General Electric (GE). GE cut their dividend after the financial meltdown in 2007-2008. And indeed, the stock did get beaten up in the short-term.

Dividends are typically paid quarterly and are favorably regarded by investors because they are considered reliable. Investors can count on their dividends for income or to help get a consistent yield on their equities. Some examples of blue chip stocks include well-known companies such as Wal-Mart, Coca-Cola, General Electric, and Exxon Mobile.

One of the measures of how the market is valuing a particular stock is its dividend yield. The math equation to calculate the dividend yield is to take the stock's annual payout and divide it by its share price. A stock's projected dividend over the next three years (PEG Ratio) greatly affects the stock's valuation, and can be used to determine if a stock is currently under or over valued.

A dividend yield that is high compared to interest rates on bonds is often the sign of a real bargain. At the time of writing of this book, the dividend yield of the average stock is, in fact, very high compared to the interest rate on US government bonds. At the very least, as of the writing of this book, yields indicate stocks offer a better value than bonds, and investors are missing a good deal if they ignore that signal. The best way to exploit this situation is to purchase a solid company that pays a consistent dividend. Consider Colgate-Palmolive with the trading symbol "CL." As you know, they are a consumer-product giant and maker of toothpaste, deodorant, detergent and many other products. They have paid big dividends without interruption since 1895 and have increased their payout annually for the past 47 years. At a share price of $74, the stock yields a 2.8% dividend. If you think that's low, think again. A 10-year treasury note, as of the date of this publication, has yielded just 2.3% and a 5-year treasury note is only 1.1%. This is all data through October 8, 2012.

## DOW JONES INDUSTRIAL AVERAGE

There are indices (plural for index) for every conceivable sector of the economy. A market index is designed to track the performance of a specific group of stocks that are considered to represent a particular market sector. The most commonly used indices include the Dow Jones Industrial Average (DJIA), New York Stock Exchange (NYSE) Composite Index, S&P 500 Composite Stock Price Index, Wilshire 500 Total Market Index, Russell 2000® Index, and Nasdaq-100 Index.

The Dow Jones Industrial Average (DJIA) consists of the common stock of 30 blue-chip stock companies such as Exxon Mobil, Verizon, General Electric, etc. You can refer to the table at the end of this section for a complete list of DJIA companies. One of the best places to look for a dividend paying blue-chip company is in the DJIA. As mentioned before, these are usually solid companies that are leaders in their industry and considered to be lower risk than the rest of the market. However, again I will stress that it should be understood that no stock is safe. It is worth noting that all 30 companies comprising this index paid a dividend with the average yield of the index paying 2.7% as of June 8, 2012. That is over 20 basis points higher than a year ago. Among the index components, Proctor and Gamble and 3M Corporation, have boosted their dividends each year for at least 50 years.

A common investor mistake is staring at the DOW ticker and assuming their portfolio is performing about the same. The Dalbar (*) study shows investor returns do not come close to outperforming the indices due to fees and bad timing decisions. <u>Remember, the indices such as the DOW or S&P 500 are unmanaged "things" that do not consider timing or expense variables that people have to in the real world. So don't be misled.</u>

To the untrained eye, the Dow can be a very deceptive index. It is a very narrow index and is only large cap. Since there are only 30 stocks that make up the Dow, it is not representative of all the stocks available to an investor. The DJIA consists of all blue-chip stocks from companies and industries that do not proportionately represent the total investment market. The fact that the DJIA is not a value-based index such as the S&P, can give an investor an inaccurate picture of the market. Value-weighted is a more accurate metric because it gives more weight to larger cap companies, whereas the DOW is simply an average. The DJIA is not designed to be representative of the entire investment market. On the other hand, the S&P 500 is an index that *is* value-weighted and is composed of 500 different large cap stocks, not 30. This index is more representative of a cross section of companies and industries.

The S&P 500 is indeed value-weighted, meaning larger companies are weighted in the formula calculating the index. Whereas, the Dow Jones is simply taking the total amount of gain or loss for the day or any given moment and dividing it by 30 (the number of companies represented in the index). An Index that is weighted is always going to be a more accurate indicator of the market it represents. The S&P 500 is probably the Index watched most by the majority of investors because it represents the largest portion of the biggest publicly traded companies in the United States domestic market.

In summary, a price-weighted index, such as the DJIA, is an index of the sum of the prices of the securities within the index divided by a predetermined divisor. In the case of the Dow, the predetermined divisor is 30, which represents the 30 blue-chip companies that comprise that Index. It is price weighted and not value weighted. It fails to reflect the payment of dividends, ignores stock dividends and is a small sample of stocks. They are all blue-chip stocks from companies and industries that do not proportionately represent the total investment market. Below is a table of all the blue-chip companies comprising the Dow.

**Table of blue-chip companies that comprise the Dow Jones Industrial Average:**

| Company Name | Ticker | Sector |
|---|---|---|
| 3M Co. | MMM | Diversified Industrials |
| Alcoa Inc. | AA | Aluminum |
| American Express Co. | AXP | Consumer Finance |
| AT&T Inc. | T | Fixed Line Telecommunications |
| Bank of America Corp. | BAC | Banks |
| Boeing Co. | BA | Aerospace |
| Caterpillar Inc. | CAT | Commercial Vehicles & Trucks |

| Company Name | Ticker | Sector |
|---|---|---|
| Chevron Corp. | CVX | Integrated Oil & Gas |
| Citigroup Inc. | C | Banks |
| Coca-Cola Co. | KO | Soft Drinks |
| E.I. DuPont de Nemours & Co. | DD | Commodity Chemicals |
| Exxon Mobil Corp. | XOM | Integrated Oil & Gas |
| General Electric Co. | GE | Diversified Industrials |
| General Motors Corp. | GM | Automobiles |
| Hewlett-Packard Co. | HPQ | Computer Hardware |
| Home Depot Inc. | HD | Home Improvement Retailers |
| Intel Corp. | INTC | Semiconductors |
| International Business Machines Corp. | IBM | Computer Services |
| Johnson & Johnson | JNJ | Pharmaceuticals |
| JPMorgan Chase & Co. | JPM | Banks |
| Kraft Foods Inc. Cl A | KFT | Food Products |
| McDonald's Corp. | MCD | Restaurants & Bars |
| Merck & Co. Inc. | MRK | Pharmaceuticals |
| Microsoft Corp. | MSFT | Software |
| Pfizer Inc. | PFE | Pharmaceuticals |
| Procter & Gamble Co. | PG | Nondurable Household Products |
| United Technologies Corp. | UTX | Aerospace |
| Verizon Communications Inc. | VZ | Fixed Line Telecommunications |
| Wal-Mart Stores Inc. | WMT | Broadline Retailers |
| Walt Disney Co. | DIS | Broadcasting & Entertainment |

## PREFERRED STOCK

Blue chip companies (and any company for that matter) can issue two types of stock: common and preferred stock. Common stock is what you see in the Dow Jones Industrial Average and in other indices such as the S&P 500. Preferred shares are another type of issue considered less volatile than the sister blue-chip common stock, but they are still an equity and they can go up or down in value.

There are four types of preferred stock: **Cumulative** – share-holders are paid missed preferred dividends before the dividends are paid on common stock; **Non-cumulative** – shareholders are not paid missed dividends; **Participating** – Shareholders receive regular fixed dividends plus an additional dividend if the common stock dividend exceeds a specified amount. **Convertible** – Shareholders can convert preferred shares into a specified number of common shares.

Preferred shares are higher on the food chain than common stock when it comes to dividends. That is, preferred stock dividends are paid out before common stock dividends. Preferred stock is often used in income portfolios for investors. With a preferred stock, you have a chance for some capital appreciation, but you typically will receive a reliable dividend for the preferred shares you own. Not every company that is traded in the exchanges also has preferred shares to offer investors. You have to look for the companies that offer preferred stock and they are not hard to find. A quick inquiry on any reliable Internet search engine should give you a list of companies that offer preferred stock.

Preferred stock pays dividends subject to declaration by the corporation. Dividends are paid on a certain percentage of the par value of the stock. Preferred share dividends must be satisfied before a company can pay dividends to holders of common stock. A company doesn't have to pay dividends, but once they start paying dividends they tend not to stop paying dividends because they don't want to give their investors the wrong or negative impression about their company. Dividends can also be issued as additional shares of stock in the company. Preferred stock holders also get preferential treatment over common stock holders in the case of a company bankruptcy or liquidation. Typically, those buying preferred shares are corporations and individuals looking for a fixed steady flow of income. Preferred stock can also be used as a bond proxy or substitute in a portfolio, often when bonds are expected to be volatile or low yielding.

# DIVIDEND REINVESTMENT PLAN (DRIPS)

A Dividend Reinvestment Plan is commonly referred to as a DRIP. The concept behind the DRIP is actually very simple. Instead of having the dividend distributed to you personally, you just opt to automatically reinvest all the dividends back into the stock to purchase more shares. Some investors like this option because you don't need a broker to do this and you don't have to pay a broker's fee. If you own the stock in a company, you can simply ask the company to reinvest all of your dividends rather than sending you a check for the dividends. Of course, you can also do this through an advisor or retail online account. Many financial advisors don't like it when people do this on their own, simply because it does not include them. You should discuss this with your financial advisor to determine the best strategy for yourself.

DRIPs can be pretty effective. Keep in mind that you still have to pay tax each year on any dividends paid out by the stock company, even if you reinvest them. All dividends are taxable, whether or not you do a DRIP. DRIPs are very similar to Dollar Cost Averaging. As you may already know, Dollar Cost Averaging is putting money into the same investment on a regular basis, theoretically paying a lower average share price. But, I stress the word theoretically. True Dollar Cost Averaging is purchasing shares on a consistent basis whether the share price is up or down. It is definitely a smarter way to gradually invest, rather than dumping your entire life savings into the market in one day.

First, you can own a stock directly from a company and sign up for a DRIP arrangement. But, I recommend opening up a TD Ameritrade or Charles Schwab account and they will reinvest dividends with no transaction costs. In one of these accounts you can have all your stocks in one reportable location for easy monitoring. These arrangements are much more convenient than owning each individual stock directly with each company.

## PROPER DIVERSIFICATION

I would like to state again that buying appropriate stocks can be a good supplement to a properly diversified portfolio. I do not recommend just having your whole life savings in just a bunch of dividend paying stocks, because you're not able to get the diversity that will get you better upside and lesser downside that you can from an indexed core portfolio. I explain in a later chapter how to create a properly diversified portfolio using the 7-Twelve method as your core and then you can surround it with a measured percentage of dividend-paying stocks. I will stress again that stocks can pay a dividend, but they can decrease in value. Keep in mind stocks are a risk instrument. There's no absolute guarantee of your principal in any way, shape, or form.

# CHAPTER 6

# THE SKINNY ON RISK AND YOUR RETIREMENT

*Living at risk is like jumping off a cliff and making your wings on the way down.*~ Ray Bradbury

*Risk comes from not knowing what you are doing.*~ Warren Buffet

The above quotes represent similar perceptions of risk. It has been interesting for me to see how people view risk as I have met with clients over the past twenty years. My experience in working with individuals with medium to wealthy portfolios has led me to the following conclusion: **Mismanagement of risk is one of the biggest causes of lost wealth.** It begs repeating: **Mismanagement of risk is one of the biggest causes of lost wealth.** This cold fact is especially true the closer you get to retirement. At or near retirement, all conditions are magnified in their impact.

### How much risk should you take AT or NEAR retirement?

As you know, the answer to that question will be somewhat different for each person. Each person is unique and has differing perceptions as well as various tolerances for risk.

However, there are a few prudent principles the pre- or post-retiree investor should know about. If they fear any risk to their future cost of living or to their future income streams, they should proceed with great caution. Interestingly enough, both the modestly wealthy and the very wealthy retirees have similar concerns about outliving their money. *With life expectancy now routinely reaching the late 80's to mid-90's and the rising cost of living, retirees now, more than ever, risk outliving their money if they are not careful.*

Based on my experience working with retirees, and those preparing for retirement, I have outlined six principles that will serve as a guide to successful retirement planning. If you take these to heart, you almost cannot fail to preserve and grow your nest egg going forward.

### PRINCIPLE 1
**When a person is at or near retirement, they become a different investor than they were before, whether they realize it or not.**

In order for the other following principles to make sense, you must be reasonable enough to agree with the above statement. If not, many more mistakes will be made going forward that may cause you to run out of money. You see, during your younger working years you are in what is called the "accumulation stage" of your investment life. When you are at or near retirement, you are in the "harvesting/preservation stage" of your investment life. These two stages are both very, very different.

The accumulation stage is typically accomplished fairly effectively for individuals primarily due to personal or company contributions to their retirement plans and the length of time for the accumulation stage, which is approximately **35 to 40 years**. Note, that I left out what the market gives and takes. This is due to the fact that employer and employee **contributions and the length of time of the accumulation stage** are the primary drivers in growing your retirement plans. In fact, equity growth can be a very small part. However, the harvesting stage is **only 20 to 30 years** if one lives long enough. The length of time you have left in the harvesting stage undeniably magnifies the impact of financial mistakes. Furthermore, in the harvesting stage, it is crucial as to how quickly a remedy for mistakes can be implemented, if and when they are uncovered.

The harvesting stage has another unique factor that cannot be ignored, which is in great contrast to the accumulation stage. The harvesting stage has the unknown, but inevitable and unpredictable challenge of failing physical and mental acuity. Most people recognize the fact that they are a different investor at or near retirement simply because of time, and they don't have time to wait for markets to recover large losses. However, you must also acknowledge that you may not always have the ability to effectively make decisions about risk because of diminished mental capacity. As an investor, a professional, and an accomplished day-trader, I sure do not want to spend my retirement watching CNBC or staring at the market with worry. Unfortunately, as we age, many people are not able to reason or handle stressful financial decisions as clearly as they had in their younger years. Judgment can be impaired when it comes to making risk decisions. Thus is the case for a structured income plan to supplement your life. As one becomes older, it is a good rule-of-thumb to try to keep some of your finances going in the direction of more simplicity rather than complexity. It makes sense, yes?

After personally meeting with several hundred investors, I have found that people who can come to terms with the first principle are more successful seniors, and have less stress than those who continue to be in denial of this reality. The good news is, probably 90% of the people I've met, after a risk discussion, will agree with this first principle. **Principle #1 is the mother of all principles. Do not even bother to read the rest of this chapter if you cannot accept Principle #1 as fact.** If you are in denial of the facts of life, you are almost guaranteed to have major headaches, and usually, at the worst possible time.

## PRINCIPLE 2
### Observe the Rule of 100 Minus Your Age

The rule of 100 is a simple way to determine if you are even in the ballpark of where you should be with your ratio of risk money to safe money. This rule is very simple. You just take the number 100 and subtract your age and the remaining number is the maximum percentage of assets you should have in risk-based investments that have the potential to lose money. For example, if you're 70 years old, you would subtract 70 from 100. The answer, 30, represents the maximum percentage amount you should have at risk. In this example, 30% is how much risk you should have at that stage of your life. If you are trying to factor this for a couple, just take the average of the two ages and subtract *that* number from 100. I realize this is not the most scientific methodology. We utilize more detailed metrics when we advise people about their investments. However, it is still a good indicator to determine if you have the proper amount at risk for your age, at least, to know if you are in the ballpark.

100 minus <u>Your Age</u> = % Risk you should have for your age

## PRINCIPLE 3
### Do not confuse Bond Income <u>Funds</u> with "Safety" or "Guarantee of Principle"

One of the most common misunderstandings is people's misguided belief that a fixed income fund is the same as a safe, principle protected investment. The truth is that bond income funds, (do not confuse with ownership of actual, individual bonds), can lose value just like any other mutual fund. In 2008, fixed income funds melted down with the rest of the fund universe, and offered no safe-haven whatsoever. Some went down drastically. **Bond <u>funds</u> are not safe**. They are just considered a more *conservative* balance in an equity/bond portfolio. Do not be among those that make this mistake. A lot of folks had a rude awakening about bond funds in Great Recession of 2008, and they will never forget that again. Also, at our current low interest rates, bonds look to be possibly the next bubble. You see, bond yields have an inverse relationship to interest rates. Our interest rates have nowhere to go but up, sometime in the not so distant future. What does that mean? It means bond yields have nowhere to go but down. In a mutual bond fund, you will get smashed. This is because bond funds have no maturities, specified income stream, no return of principal, and after big fund outflows, those that stay in the bond fund will be greatly damaged for staying in the bond fund. Their values will drop significantly. In bond funds or any mutual fund, your ongoing loyalty by staying in the fund is rewarded with punishment.

If you own an actual bond, and not a bond fund, you will not lose your principal, assuming the individual company does not go bankrupt. Your bond's coupon payment will still come every six months, and barring a company bankruptcy, you will get your original principal back at maturity. The calculated yield will dip with the rest in the interim, but you will not realize the loss, unless you redeem the bond prior to maturity.

## What IS guaranteed?

The only things that are absolutely guaranteed are government-backed securities such as Treasury Bills, Notes, and Bonds. Treasury Inflation Protected Securities (TIPS), Treasuries, Ginnie Mae's, Freddie Mac's are also backed by the full faith and credit of the US Government. Other guaranteed vehicles are CD's and savings accounts at banks that are FDIC insured up to $250,000. Also, fixed and indexed annuities can be added to this list of safe options. These are called GICs or Guaranteed Insurance Contracts (this list is not exhaustive). GICS are backed by the company itself, they are often reinsured, and each state has its own Guaranty Association such as Ohio which will cover $250,000 per annuity company per person. All of the above categories are the only truly safe instruments that are guaranteed by some institution or authority. So, don't make the mistake by thinking if you have a fixed income fund, you are not in the market. That is absolutely not true. Anything that is a "fund," unless it is a fund that has only government guaranteed contracts, can go down in value.

## PRINCIPLE 4
### Have Recurring Risk Discussions with Yourself as Well as With a Qualified Financial Advisor

The basis of this principle is many people do not even participate in a risk discussion at all. Some only get a risk assessment in the beginning of a relationship with an advisor. However, risk discussions should take place at the beginning and be recurring throughout your investment life. We all face transitions in life such as age, financial status, ability to work, our goals, and the list can go on and on. Any life change can affect your financial plan and must be discussed on a regular basis.

Not only should you have this conversation with a trusted investment advisor, but you also need to try to understand yourself as best you can. You need to have a recurring conversation with yourself. How do you really feel about risk? Do you really understand risk? Do you understand that not all financial investments are equal in risk? After an introspective conversation with yourself, you should continue the dialogue with a qualified financial advisor to adjust your investment portfolio and make it reflective of your changing risk tolerance.

*There are many studies that show there is __not__ an equal amount of emotion when you lose 20% in the market as compared to gaining 20% in the market. In other words, it is a proven fact that the joy of the gain is not equally as deep as the pain of loss. Studies show that people feel loss far more emotionally, and for a longer duration than they do with wins. Make sure your investments reflect you... The real you!*

## PRINCIPLE 5
### Avoid the Equally Dangerous Over-Diversification
### or the Redundancy Portfolio

On one end of the spectrum, having only one or two asset classes represented in your portfolio can be a very risky proposition. But a portfolio with too many positions can be just as risky with your nest egg. I am describing two extremes that have equal dangers to you.

Allow me to explain. I can't tell you how many $200,000 and $400,000 portfolios I have reviewed over the years that have 50 and 60 stock positions in just large cap funds. People will say, "Well, I have different industries across the large cap asset class." That is true. But they are all "Large Cap Assets," and therefore, under-diversified. It is a nightmare to analyze these "haystack" or "linguini" portfolios. Very often they own positions that have only $1,500 to $2,000 in each position. Interestingly enough, often these models are regularly created by the large brokerage companies. The reasoning behind the haystack or linguini portfolio is to throw enough large cap funds on the wall, for then, something is bound to make money. Or, the client can't sue the advisor for having money in the case of another Enron, so lets just put a million stocks in one portfolio. I call this over-diversified financial plan a "linguini portfolio," because, if you throw enough linguini on the wall, some of it is going to stick. But, most of it is going to fall to ground. I feel these linguini portfolios display a lack of education, conviction, and ideas. I suspect these designs may even be legally motivated. If you have 8 million different stocks, it may be harder to sue an advisor for losses.

The linguini portfolio is typically in a bunch of large cap stocks even though they are often in multiple industries such as medical, agricultural, etc. The rising tide raises all boats in a certain asset class, but it can also sink all the boats as well. In a down market, what do you sell? So, you want to have yourself in the right amount of asset classes, but not in so many that you are so spread apart that you can't have any control over it. You don't want to be so out of whack that you risk getting wiped out by the next inevitable market cycle playing itself out.

Actually, you should be able to explain your portfolio design in one or two sentences. A good succinct description would be, "My accounts are comprised of all twelve asset classes in over 40 countries and are rebalanced." It can be as simple as that. There is no way to accurately and succinctly describe a linguini portfolio, except maybe… "I have a linguini portfolio."

This leads us to the question, when is too much diversification really just too much, and nothing more than duplication and redundancy? When your portfolio is over or improperly diversified, there is always a curve that leads to diminishing returns. If you have a $200,000 portfolio with 50 stocks in it, which is very common, and one of them goes up 10%, what impact is that really making in a positive way in your portfolio? When 20 others have gone down? Or, when the market is making a huge correction, like it does periodically as part of its nature, what do you sell? You're going to face a lot of transaction costs to get rid of the stocks while trying to reduce your risk exposure.

The linguini portfolio screams of an advisor who doesn't want to take responsibility for any kind of choices within their design. Just having more "stuff" does not make proper diversification. So, avoid the linguini portfolio because it can be just as damaging as an under-diversified portfolio, as it is an extreme. And we know extremes do not last very long. In the next chapter, I will explain what and how you can simply reach optimal diversification.

### PRINCIPLE 6
#### Utilize Low and Zero Correlation of Assets
#### to Reduce Downside and Improve Upside

People often conclude that if they have reduced the downside, they are automatically conceding upside potential. I can tell you without a doubt it is utterly untrue. First, I must explain what "correlation" means, for those that are not familiar with quantitative or statistical analysis. The range here is from -1 to +1. Those two ends of the spectrum represent the maximum difference between two investments. In other words, if something is equally correlated, that is, if you have one investment that is exactly the same as another investment in the same asset class, they will have a +1 relationship or correlation with each other. Whereas, an investment that is exactly the opposite in correlation to another investment will have a -1 relationship. You don't want half of your portfolio to be +1's and the other half to be -1's, because one set of investments will be going up and the other set will be going down by the same amount all the time. You would always have a draw. That wouldn't make a lot of sense. What you should be trying to accomplish is to get your assets as close to zero (in between -1 and +1) as possible. I will discuss this in greater depth in the chapter 8, the **7-Twelve: The Broad Diversification Portfolio.**

It's not effective to have too many of the same things. Many people have mutual funds or stocks that are all large cap, but that's only one of twelve asset classes. This person's portfolio is going to live and die with large cap. In the last 10 years, the S&P 500 has returned <u>negative one half of one percent</u>. So, the goal is to have assets that have less and less relation to one another. For instance, having a Guaranteed Insurance Contract (GIC) in relationship to your stock portfolio. There is absolutely zero correlation between the GIC and the market. They are both very different. You can also go further to improve the asset balance in your equity portfolio. You can have exposure to all twelve-asset classes, at all times, so you don't get the big drawdowns and you do not have to chase trends. <u>Believe it or not, statistics show that with the right sweet spot of diversification, you can actually have higher upside compared to the downside.</u>

## CONCLUSION

Once you have clearly understood and calibrated your risk vs. safe money ratio, you can ignore all the financial fear mongering you hear and the plethora of television and radio advertisements that guide you to their supposed solution. There is a continuous flow of radio advertising, leading you to believe that things such as gold will bullet proof your IRA. Bullet proof? Really? These commercials are simply misleading and should be censured. In my opinion, the SEC is currently very overwhelmed and slimmed down. In my opinion, the SEC does not enforce enough existing regulations to protect investors. The SEC and Congress have failed to protect investors from the fraud of the 80's and 90's as well as the most recent cataclysmic events beginning in 2008.

I will get off my soapbox now and finish this chapter with one thought. By balancing risk, you can be both a long-term investor **and** a bird-in-the-hand investor at the same time. That is how you come to grips with Principal #1.

A balanced, hybrid approach to risk and income sources puts you in the position of not having to bet that you are right. But, it puts you in the camp of just betting you won't be wrong. Think about it.

Low correlation between your assets can be done very easily, so you do not need to be a rocket scientist. I apologize for being so technical in certain spots of this book. In order to be responsible and credible, some things must be taught. But you should at least understand the general concept that you want each piece of your nest egg to have a measured difference from the other in behavior, quality, and cycles. The result is higher upside as compared to downside. Actually, I probably could have made this whole chapter this paragraph. Oh well.

In chapter 8, I will describe the Broad Diversification model that was developed by Dr. Craig Israelson, a full-time professor at Bringham Young University. His model and others like it that we use solve for the diversification question, and take all of the speculation out of investing.

# CHAPTER 7

# THE SKINNY ON EXCHANGE TRADED FUNDS (ETF'S) AND INDEXING

*Attempting to forecast whether the market is at a peak
or in a valley—and whether to buy or sell stocks as a result—
is a waste of time. I don't know anyone who has been right
more than once in a row.* ~ Legendary Investor Peter Lynch

*After 50 years in the business, I do not know of anybody who
has done it (market timing) successfully and consistently. I do not
even know anybody who knows anybody who has done it successfully
and consistently* ~ John Bogle, Founder, Vanguard Funds

**Markets build people's wealth. Advisors and fund managers
do not. Myself included.**

Because we have such an efficient market, it is virtually impossible to consistently beat the market. That's why low costs and indexing, as well as not trying to outsmart it, can provide superior returns to speculation and gambling with your money. According to Nobel Prize Winner Harry Markowitz, his Efficient Market Hypothesis states the market's movements reflect all known information about a stock on a constant and continuous basis. In other words, there is little or no proven ability to anticipate the future movement of a stock or the market itself.

## What is the difference between actively managed funds and indexing?

In recent years, Exchange Traded Funds (ETF) gained great popularity among savvy investors and are over $1 trillion in assets. The traditional mutual fund's efficacy is being greatly challenged by the growing ETF movement. Because there are distinct advantages to ETF's as compared to mutual funds, ETF's take an index-related approach to investing, whereas, most mutual funds are managed funds directed by money managers. These managers use their own judgment and experience to make deliberate choices about which investments to include in a particular fund. Part of Mark Matson's ($4 billion under management) philosophy about Wall Street bullies speaks to active management. He explains how these gurus always want you to think they are smarter than you. I can tell you first hand that they are dead wrong!

You may be interested to know that over <u>90% of actively managed funds DO NOT beat the market</u>. Furthermore, active mutual funds have both visible and invisible fees, costs, and charges. The small percentage of most active managers that beat the market in a given year or years, do so simply by luck due to the fact that they are buoyed by the performance of the core asset class. In other words, many people get sucked into the 10% of funds that have beaten the market and make the mistake of buying these past returns. This is called chasing returns. The value of funds WILL pivot downward when money starts to flow out of the asset class. Funds that do well for a year or two are largely due to the cyclical nature of various asset classes. I strongly recommend that you do not get caught in this trap.

Here is a list of why mutual funds are not the investment vehicle of choice for enlightened advisors and clients:

1. Most people have no clue as to their cost of capital in an active fund (first step Morningstar).

2. Over 90% of active funds do not beat the indices.

3. The modern efficiency of our markets, make it nearly impossible to beat the market for any prolonged period of time by active lane jumping and preemptive predictions.

4. In non-IRA accounts, active mutual funds can produce "phantom income" (described in chapter one).

5. The investors that stay in a fund have an additional risk if others have bailed out of a fund for any reason. When investors flow out of a fund, those that stay put get penalized in the form of diminished equity.

6. There is a lack of transparency. In a mutual fund, the investor has no idea where their money is being invested on any given day.

7. The investor generally has no control over the six items above.

## What is Indexing?

The great John Bogle, one of the founders of Vanguard, has held a long-time belief of not fighting the efficiency of the market with active trend following or stock picking. He asserts in several books that active management is for the birds. He, others, and I believe in three primary principals:

1. Keep your investment costs low.

2. Indexing beats active stock picking. Markets make money. People don't!

3. Don't chase asset classes. Be in all of them at the same time and rebalance.

John Bogle is one of the originators of the first indexed mutual funds at Vanguard. These indexed funds were low in costs, had little turnover, and were 100% transparent. They also outperformed most active funds and are still around today. Those first "indexed" mutual funds were the precursor to what we now know as an ETF or Exchange Traded Fund.

## What exactly is an ETF?

An ETF is like a basket of stocks in one position. For example, an S&P 500 ETF has 500 stocks in it. A small-cap index may have the 2000 small companies from the Russell 2000 index. There are thousands of ETF's out there now to index to nearly everything. For example, if you want to index gold, you can buy a gold ETF. If you want to include a China index, one ETF can satisfy this with a multi-industry China index. Exchange Traded Funds are simple, visible, and tax-efficient.

Here is a non-exhaustive list of single ETF asset classes:

1. Large, Mid, Small, and Microcap
2. Currencies
3. Precious Metals
4. Countries (Brazil, China, Japan, etc.)
5. Bonds
6. Inverted (they go up when an index goes down)
7. Commodities (gold, silver, oil, wheat, cattle, etc.)
8. Industry Groups (technology, durable goods, consumer staples, biotech, etc.)
9. Natural Resources

Another important point about ETF's is that they trade in real time like stocks. You can use charts to assist in better entries and exits. Mutual funds do not have charts and they are priced only once per business day at 5:30 p.m.

## How do I know what ETF's to buy?

Before you look for specific ETF's, you need to settle on an objective or design of a portfolio. In the next chapter I will explain one such design called the 7Twelve "multi-asset portfolio." So, the design comes first, and then you decide what indexes you want in the portfolio. From there it is plug and chug.

### Is the track record of an ETF important?

No. Because if you see a negative return on an ETF over some arbitrary time period, it just simply means that sector, asset class, or segment of the market just had the inevitable cyclical downside. <u>There is no management error for one to judge in an ETF.</u> The history of an ETF is basically irrelevant. The history is a history of an asset class, not a management company. Why is this so? Because, an ETF should be used with other ETF's in a portfolio. A portfolio should be designed with a strategy. Therefore, you need to see a track record of a proposed portfolio design. You do not want all of your investments to go up or down all at the same time. That would be terrible risk management and an opportunity cost as well.

As I have said, every asset class has its day in the sun and its day in the rain. Even professionals cannot predict asset class cycles consistently. Our market works too efficiently to beat it. One does not know that something is a strong positive or negative trend until it is in your rear-view mirror. That is why passive indexing across all asset classes eliminates the inevitable human error in trying to time or predict trends. It is as simple as that<u>. How do you match or beat the market? You *become* the market and rebalance. That's it.</u>

### What are the costs in an ETF?

<u>**Exchange Traded Funds have no loads or commissions.**</u>
That is why working with a fee-based advisor saves you money each and every year, if nothing else, thus directionally aiding positive returns. This is assuming, of course, that the fee-based advisor is not charging more than 1-1.4% in total costs. On the other hand, loaded, or commissioned-based mutual funds involve commissions, which cost investors plenty.

ETF annual charges are pretty low, usually less than ½ of 1%. If you work with a fee-based advisor charging 1% to manage your portfolio, your total investment costs should not exceed 1.4% per year (ETF annual costs included).

On the other hand, the average mutual fund holder has 2% or higher annual fees. Realistically, your costs in a mutual fund or variable annuity can be as high as 3-5% per year.

### Are ETF's tax-efficient?

ETF's are more tax efficient than active mutual funds. They do not create phantom income tax and the capital gains are deferred like a stock, until you decide to trigger the capital gain, which means more control for you. Also, dividends from ETF's may receive preferential tax treatment like stocks.

### Do you have more control in an ETF or an active mutual fund?

The empowerment for investors in ETF's begins and ends with transparency. When you invest in an ETF, you know exactly what and where your money is at all times. If you have a position in the S&P 500 Index ETF, then you know exactly where your money is invested and you can see it clearly. Lack of transparency in active mutual funds is a growing problem for investors. People want, and should have, more transparency about where their money is and what the costs are in their portfolio.

Another investor empowerment from ETF's comes in the form of being able to slowly construct a new portfolio over time. You do not want your money to be invested all in one day. If you do, you run the short-term risk of getting "whipsawed" in the short-term, by market volatility. A portfolio should be built like a house with one ETF foundation block at a time. Conversely, if the market is melting down and you want to reduce your exposure, you can remove some of the more volatile pieces.

Did you ever wonder why a commissioned-based advisor plunks you in all of the mutual funds in one day? The answer is simple. The advisor does not get paid until your funds are invested in the market. The commissioned broker, from the start, is putting your money in the market in one day, even if that might be the worst day of the month or year to commit your life savings to the market.

Have you ever wondered why you get so much attention from a commission-based advisor in the beginning and then you get less and less attention as time goes on? This phenomenon occurs because the advisor has already made his money off of you and receives little or no recurring income annually. Think about it! Where would you put your attention if you were them? Strictly "new business," that's where.

## A Final Word on Exchange Traded Funds:

ETF's are why the more discerning advisors are able to keep their clients' costs and taxes under control. ETF's have negligible turnover (in contrast to active mutual funds), no active market timing, bare minimum costs, high tax efficiency, transparency, are indexed based and are not dependent on market timing.

Additionally, ETF's do not generate Phantom Income, or runaway taxation. ETF's can receive preferential (lower) dividend tax treatment, so they are great for non-IRA accounts due to their superior tax efficiency compared to active mutual funds.

Your portfolio performance potential really lies in the *design* of the portfolio, not in just one or two specific positions. You do not want all of your positions in an account to go up at the same time because that means you are not diversified. The 7Twelve design discussed in the next chapter is an example of broad diversification. This is due to the average, low-correlation (0.40) of each building block in the design. You may want to re-read the prior chapter on risk and correlation to deepen your understanding of the concept of correlation and what it means to YOUR money. It is imperative to understand that low-correlated assets better protect your nest egg.

## CHAPTER 8

# THE SKINNY ON THE 7TWELVE® BROAD DIVERSIFICATION DESIGN[1]

In chapter six, I shared with you important facts about risk and the price paid for heavy risk-taking. This chapter covers one of the best ways for a retiree to be properly diversified – not under or even over-diversified. Remember, each extreme can be equally detrimental to your nest egg.

I have found the 7Twelve® Broad Diversification Design to be a highly effective model to attain consistent returns on the upside, while minimizing the downside of an investment portfolio. In 2006, I was reading one of my trade journals and an article caught my eye. It was an article by Dr. Craig Israelsen, PhD, who is a full-time faculty member at Brigham Young University. Craig had been analyzing mutual funds for many years as well as teaching family financial planning at BYU. He also has written articles for all of the major financial publications such as *Money, Wall Street Journal, Forbes, Investment Advisor Magazine*, and others.

I was so intrigued by the logic and elegant simplicity of the 7Twelve, that I read the initial article over several times. This relatively simple, tax-efficient, low-cost, optimum diversification portfolio design instantly caught my attention and has held

---

\* 7Twelve® is a registered trademark of Craig L. Israelsen.

my interest ever since. After the third article run-through, I got the daring idea to "Google" Dr. Israelsen and give him a call. I called him, and much to my surprise, he picked up the phone in his office. We started talking and the rest is history. I made a friend that day and the 7Twelve design has been at the basic core of my firm's money management system ever since.

I want to preface the explanation of the 7Twelve concept with this thought: The 7Twelve is a total portfolio design consisting of 12 positions, which together, can be modified or integrated with nearly any other design. It is not a product. It can be constructed with Exchange-Traded Funds (ETF's) or mutual funds. I prefer the ETF's due to the low-cost, ease of control, transparency, and preferential tax treatment (in non-IRA accounts). The mutual fund version of the 7Twelve, albeit good, is still bridled with tax inefficiencies, lack of transparency, and the costs of turnover inherent in mutual funds. While index mutual funds are pretty lean on costs compared to many active funds, for practicality and precision, I prefer the passive or ETF version of the 7Twelve, as opposed to the equally performing active 7Twelve using indexed mutual funds.

Many of the important qualities any prudent financial planner considers or desires for his clients can be accomplished within the 7Twelve design.

These factors or qualities are:

1. Ease of tracking (when used with Exchange-Traded Funds)

2. The ability to build each block of the 7Twelve foundation carefully and gradually to avoid early market risk or reduce a portfolio's exposure to risk when conditions warrant

3. Reasonably simple to understand

4. Exceptional performance history and a lesser downside in bear markets

5. 100% transparency for both the advisor and the client (knowing where your money is and exactly how it is invested)

6. Low investment cost structure (only available with fee-based advisors)

7. Tax-efficiency (When used with Exchange-Traded Funds)

8. No hidden fees

There is no perfect design or product. No single financial product or strategy can be an "end all" total solution by itself for growing and preserving your nest egg. In a nutshell, successful financial planning is the result of having several sub-strategies within your entire portfolio.

## What is the "Seven" in 7Twelve?

Dr. Israelsen came to the design of the 7Twelve by analyzing the historic returns of the seven core asset classes. Any money invested can be categorized into one of the above seven core asset classes. The classes are as follows:

1. US Stocks

2. Non-US Stocks

3. Real Estate

4. Resources

5. US Bonds

6. Non-US Bonds

7. Cash

Dr. Israelsen carefully reviewed the returns of the seven asset classes over forty years. Each asset class had, at times, incredibly good and incredibly bad years, as well as everything in between. But when he back-tested the seven classes all together, the performance was superior to any of the individual assets' historical returns. When reviewing his annual report of returns you see something extraordinary, you observe great upside with a disproportionately lesser downside. There you have it. <u>Broad diversification not only reduces downside risk, but also enhances annual returns.</u> The last ten years of the

7Twelve design (passive version) has an average annualized return of over 8% per year.

## What is the "Twelve" in the "7Twelve?"

When building on the "seven core assets" concept, Dr. Israelsen felt that there were actually twelve assets needed to more accurately represent the diversity of the seven assets. Allow me to illustrate:

a) There is not just one class of US stock. There are large cap, mid-cap, and small-cap US Stocks.

b) There are two distinct classes for Non-US stock: Emerging Markets and Developing Markets.

c) The Real Estate position can be satisfied with the global REIT ETF (Real Estate Investment Trust Exchange Traded Funds).

d) There are two kinds of Resources: Commodities and Energy.

e) There are two US Bond proxies: Aggregate US Bond Index and TIPS (US Inflation Protected Treasuries).

f) And finally, just one can cover the Non-US bond index.

Over my years as a financial practitioner, I cannot tell you how many people out there are missing 3-5 of the core asset classes represented in their mutual fund or ETF portfolios. **You see folks, just because a portfolio has a bunch of "stuff" in it, does not mean you are properly diversified to reduce and get more return over time.**

There you have it. The list below consists of the twelve positions that represent the diversity of the seven basic core asset classes. With this ongoing diversification, there is no need to chase trends or be "Johnnie come lately" when it comes to getting into the current trend before it's too late.

S&P 500 Large-Cap Stock Index (500 stocks in 1 ETF)

S&P 400 Mid-Cap Stock Index (400 stocks in 1 ETF)

Vanguard Small-Cap Index (2,000 stocks in 1 ETF)

I-shares Emerging Markets (many stocks in 1 ETF)

Vanguard World Index (many developing stocks in 1 ETF)

Vanguard REIT index (25% US 75% Global REITs in 1 ETF)

I-shares SP North America Natural resources (energy index many stocks in 1 ETF)

Powershares DB Commodity Index (gold, silver, wheat, and other in 1 ETF)

Barclay's Aggregate Bond Index

US Inflation Protected Treasuries

Money Market

You can obviously tweak the 7Twelve design to suit your tastes. The design is great as a core in nearly any portfolio. **The 7Twelve design, in fact, has been designated a "prudent man design" from the Federal Pension Protection Act of 2006**. You can add as many other variables as you desire. There is always more than one way to skin a cat. Sorry Fluffy.

### Why is indexing so popular with financial advisors?

It is a proven fact that the majority of highly paid mutual fund managers are outperformed year after year by indices. The reasons for their underperformance are:

1. Timing the market on a continual basis is a risky proposition in and of itself. The "big money" institutions are finding greater and greater difficulty in actively beating the market.

2. The markets are more volatile now than ever due to computerized "high speed trading" – where thousands of trades churn over in micro=seconds and do not follow strictly to older established chart patterns. High speed trading is giving institutions fits when trying to time the market.

3. The high cost of turnover. Turnover is when fund managers replace their holdings with new holdings over and over during a current year. The enormous pressure placed on managers to deliver and compete sometimes causes over-trading which just adds to the cost of the fund (thus lowering your returns). In plain English, you keep less of YOUR money with a fund that has high turnover. Knowing your true expenses or "cost of capital" is a crucial and critical fact you must know.

Many fund managers scurry at the end of a quarter to end the period holding popular names to remain attractive to new investors. "Window dressing" for earnings season is not in the best interest of the individual mutual fund holder and is merely a job-retention strategy for the manager.

**What are the approximate expenses to an investor in the 7Twelve ETF portfolio?**

As an investor, you should expect and insist upon full transparency and clarity. You should not have to pay a fee-based advisor more than one percent (1%) per year to manage your money. Yes, I said "fee-based advisor." Fee-based advisors do not use loaded funds or funds with sales charges. But beware, there are fee-based advisors out there that are dually registered to charge a fee *and* use commissionable securities. This arrangement defeats the purpose of using a fee-based manager and really can increase your costs.

I recommend you stay away from those "double-dippers." They are no better for you than a commissioned-based advisor. You should have a fee-only advisor for 1% and your ETF costs in the 7Twleve design should amount to less than 3/10ths of 1 percent. So, your total costs should not exceed 1.3%. The average mutual fund investor has costs in *excess* of 2% annually.

Ironically, I have observed an interesting phenomenon. When I have explained the low-cost and transparent approach to some folks, they actually find it hard to believe. The public is so conditioned to accept being left in the dark by advisors, that when you show them the light, they almost become blinded by the truth. It is like the old fable of the man who lived in the darkness of the cave for his whole life, but when someone showed him the way out of the cave into light, he covered his eyes and became fearful and ran back into the cave. Darkness was what he was accustomed to and anything other that made him extremely apprehensive. It is the same thing as when someone grows up with abuse and gets conditioned to associating love with anger. It is bad, but it is all they know. Fortunately, I see this happening less and less often due to proper financial education seeping into the public consciousness.

## What has been the performance of the 7Twelve* Passive Portfolio?

Each and every year, the creator of the 7Twelve issues an updated performance report. Not only does he report the performance, but he also includes all of the things an investor should know, such as performance benchmarking, historical returns, standard deviation (the amount of swing up or down over the period), expenses, and even the average correlation of the individual components of the 7Twelve.

Surveys show that investors want more transparency regarding their money and the devil is in the details of the real annual costs of their investments. The empirical data provided by the 7Twelve annual report is 100% transparent.

## Where can I learn more about 7Twelve* and Broad Diversification?

In 2010, Dr. Craig Israelsen published a book entitled, "7Twelve: A Diversified Investment Portfolio with a Plan." This book is written in a very understandable way and is very easy for today's investors to grasp. The book describes in great detail all aspects of the design.

## Has the 7Twelve* been validated by others?

The answer to this question is a definitive "Yes." My firm is just one of many across the country that utilizes the 7Twelve in some form or another. More importantly, the 7Twelve design has been classified a "prudent man design" by the Federal Pension Protection Act of 2006. In turn, this qualifies it as a prudent design for company-sponsored retirement plans such as 401(k)'s.

## Is the 7Twelve* Best Used in the Accumulation Stage or the Harvesting/Distribution Stage?

The answer is both. Not only are the returns documented for accumulation, but Dr. Israelsen also includes a distribution section in the annual reports, which are based on actual historical returns.

As I said earlier, there is no perfect investment. However, I consider the 7Twelve to be ideal as a core design for the market side of your portfolio. It has served my clients as well as myself personally through some turbulent years. In 2008, for example, the design had negatives that were less than half of the market's losses that year.

Broad diversification is how you get consistently above-average returns with less downside. That is one of the ways you can systematically grow and protect your nest egg.

* 7Twelve® is a registered trademark of Craig L. Israelsen.

## THE *7TWELVE*® PORTFOLIO MODEL

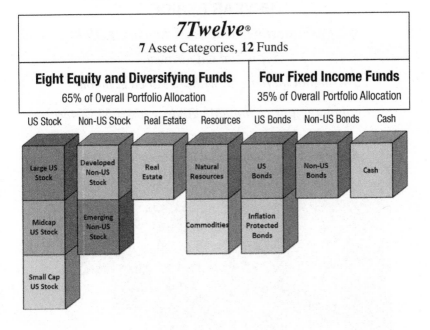

*7Twelve® is a registered trademark of Craig L. Israelsen*

## *7TWELVE*® DISTRIBUTION PORTFOLIO
## 15-YEAR PERIOD

*$250,000 starting balance on January 1, 1998*

*5% initial withdrawal*

*3% annual increase in withdrawal cash amount*

*Total amount of 15 annual withdrawals = $232,486*

**Ending Account Balance on December 31, 2012**
Assuming Annual Rebalancing

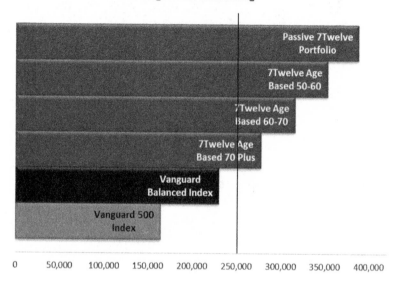

*7Twelve® is a registered trademark of Craig L. Israelsen*

# CHAPTER 9

# THE SKINNY ON ANNUITIES: Are they Good or Bad?

If you are a retiree or pre-retiree, you may have already been bombarded on a regular basis with annuity salespeople. Due to a high level of curiosity and a multitude of decisions required when approaching or living in retirement, annuities have become a very hot topic these days.

This chapter will hopefully clarify which types of annuities are suitable for your needs. In fact, some people can do without any annuities at all in their retirement portfolio and still not outlive their money. Each individual should engage in a private series of meetings with a qualified financial advisor to determine the appropriateness of annuities for their portfolio.

I wish to be upfront with readers. In our firm, we not only manage market money, we also use annuities where appropriate, when it is a good fit and in the best interest of the client. However, there are certain types of annuities we do not use because of less-than-desirable features or conditions. I will describe the two general types of annuities. After you read it for yourself, then you be the judge. You will know by the end of this chapter as to which kind, if any, may be best suited for you and yours. When all is said and done, you should still consult with a seasoned professional before going into a new contract. So here's the "skinny" on annuities.

There are two general types of annuities: **Fixed and Variable.**

## FIXED AND FIXED INDEXED ANNUITIES (FIA'S)

**Fixed** annuities are insurance-only products. They include simple interest-bearing (CD-like) products, immediate annuities (which pay out right away), and fixed-indexed annuities or sometimes called a "hybrid annuity." Call it what you will, but it is technically a fixed indexed annuity. In the financial services industry, fixed annuities are referred to as "GIC's or Guaranteed Insurance Contracts.

Fixed Annuities and Fixed Indexed Annuities are not invested in the market, and are not subject to market risk or loss of principal. FIA's do not typically have any costs in their base products. These vehicles credit interest or structured index gains to the principal and are added to principal each year. Some products have an option to choose an income rider, an enhanced death benefit rider, or a return of premium rider. These riders are optional and the costs for the riders are usually quite minimal, usually less than 1% per year. There are no other costs or fees in the average FIA.

In an indexed annuity, you can allocate your potential gains on your principal at no risk to your principal investment. Most contracts allow annuity holders to readjust their choices of interest or index option on every anniversary from the date the annuity was opened. Every company has various caps, or no caps, and indexing options. Indexing options include, but are not limited to, annual point-to-point, monthly P-T-P, monthly sum, monthly average and yearly average.

Each company must offer a detailed product brochure and statement of understanding to help a potential investor determine if any particular annuity is right for them. There are many designs and nuances with how each company credits or limits indexed gains. In my practice, we use FIA's for what I feel is their strong suit: Annual inflation rollups and income that will last a lifetime. Only when a client is very wealthy, or we are running out of safe places to put money, do we park some money in an FIA, more for safety and minor gains than anything else.

### Are Fixed Annuities and FIA's good for wealth accumulation?

Actually, I do not usually favor fixed annuities or FIA's, in most cases, purely as an accumulation vehicle. Once again, fixed annuities are the strongest for permanent income that never runs out. For folks who want safe money with low expectations, FIA's can be a good proxy for a safe accumulation vehicle. You have principal protection with potential interest or index gains. However, annuity salespeople often overstate to the public the upside potential of FIA's. There are only a few annuity companies that have no annual caps on the upside, but most are adding more and more caps, thus diluting the upside potential.

### What is typically the best use of fixed annuities or FIA's?

Income is the most ideal use of a fixed annuity as well as an indexed FIA. But, the income does not come from the base product of an FIA. FIA's have an income rider option that will grow your "income account" for a current or future income stream at an accelerated or inflated rate. This rate is predetermined and guaranteed by an insurance company before you put your money there. Simply stated: the FIA's strength is **safety and income.**

For example, an income rider is a promise to *inflate* your income account at a rate of 7% per year, until one triggers a single or joint income for life. The lifetime-income derived from these products is known in advance and should be viewed prior to choosing any financial or insurance product(s). Also, the income from these riders will pay as long as you and your spouse live – even if there is no cash left in the account during your lifetime(s). In essence, you are acquiring a personal pension when using an income rider attached to an FIA. However, unlike the employer-sponsored pensions, you can leave a remainder benefit to non-spouses, and you never relinquish ownership.

Many contracts pay out for two lives, and if even one of the two lives over 85ish, there will be no physical money left. Yet, the company has promised to pay. This is when you get into the insurance company's pocket and your rate of return then skyrockets.

With life expectancies easily reaching 90 years of age, lifetime income planning is a must for many people. The new life expectancy paradigm states, if a couple reaches the age of 60, then the chances of one of them living until 90 are very high. Plan on living, not dying.

## VARIABLE ANNUITIES

**Variable** annuities, or VA's, are both an insurance product and a registered securities product. There are several important things you should know about variable annuities. Variable Annuities or VA's are invested in the market and are subject to loss as well as gain. VA's have heavy insurance and investment costs. Over the past 20 years I have analyzed several hundred variable annuity contracts. I have found the average variable annuity has annual expenses of 3.5%, and sometimes even as high as 5%. Yes, 5%.

Variable annuities are especially bad for IRA's. Paying insurance costs on an IRA is an awful idea. An IRA does not need insurance!

Here is an example of the total costs that must be accounted for in any variable annuity:

1) **M&E annual cost:** This benefit stands for Mortality and Expenses. This cost is usually at least 1.25% to 1.50% on the whole account each and every year. Although they use the

term "M&E," this cost is simply very expensive life insurance. Allow me to give you an example of how the M&E benefit works:

## M & E Scenario:

*Initial VA account value starts at $100,000.*

*The market value later rises to $110,000 (this is your "death benefit," or "high watermark," which is the amount of money your heirs would receive when you die).*

*Some time later, the market value drifts back down below the $110,000.*

## The Result:

- If the owner dies at this point then his heirs will get the high watermark of $110,000 as a death benefit. In this case, $100K is what heirs would have received in any event. But the M&E only produces a measly $10,000 of additional benefit to the family at a cost of $1,300 per year. M&E is simply a high premium life insurance with a very low benefit.

- Stated again, M&E is purely a life insurance cost in the VA and ONLY ON THE DIFFERENCE BEWTEEN THE CURRENT VALUE AT DEATH AND THE HIGH WATERMARK.

- M&E does NOT benefit the living owner of the variable annuity. The owner must die for the benefit to be realized.

2) **Internal sub-account fees:** Sub-accounts are basically mutual fund clones inside VA's. These costs will vary greatly depending on what asset classes the sub-account is a part. Global spread costs 3-5 times the cost on turnover in US large cap, for instance. But, 2%+ annual costs would not be an exaggeration of the average. These are the operating costs of the internal funds or sub-accounts, just like any other fund.

3) **Turnover costs:** Each sub-account reports its annual turnover. If your turnover is 100%, add another 1.5% of annual costs

to the tally. If global funds, which have widespread costs to the fund, the percentage expense can be as high as 5-8% with 100% turnover. The percentages used here to measure costs for turnover are low–end estimates of how much turnover charges cost mutual fund holders every year.

4) **Optional Riders:** Income riders are often improperly interpreted for buyers of these products. These income riders typically cost around 1.5% or more per year, in addition to the above costs. I cannot tell you how many times I have heard potential clients tell me the same story about how they were told by an advisor that they could never lose money in a variable annuity because of the rider. The variable annuity "salesperson" is often very quick to emphasize the product's potential upside, but they are much less enthusiastic about revealing to the investor the high costs related to this product.

**Summary of Variable Annuity Annual Charges Based on the Above Examples:**

(Note: these costs are hypothetical based on averages we have routinely observed over 20 years in practice. Your VA may have lower or higher annual costs.)

| | |
|---|---|
| M&E | 1.25 % |
| Fund Costs | 2.00 % |
| Turnover | 0.75 %(let's use a low example here) |
| Running Total = 4.00 % | |

However, if you add an income rider that would be another 1.5% per year, bringing your total annual costs to a whopping 5.5%! Yikes!!

These costs are primarily why so many variable annuity owners watch account values treading water year after year, instead of benefiting from the cyclical bull-runs in the market. Think about it. How can an investment get anywhere, when facing a 4% annual headwind of resistance? In other words, if your costs are 4%, you need to make 4% before you even break-even in a given year. Isn't investing hard enough? Do we need to make it even harder?

**If you say VA's are so unfavorable, then why are billions of dollars put into them each year by some of the biggest companies?**

The answer to that lies in the "great deception" of Wall Street, only proven by the devastation they have wrought over the years on unsuspecting investors.

Just because a company is large, does not mean they use products or designs that are ideal and cost-effective for the public. Do I need to remind you of the now defunct brokerage houses that plowed over their very own clients in the financial meltdown? It is a public fact that Merrill Lynch sold their own bad paper during the 2008 meltdown. They did this by selling all of their shares before their clients, thus driving the unit prices down, and only then told their clients to get out. Some of the biggest financial companies are nothing more than mega-marketing machines that put out these products, which are sold before you catch on to the details. Bottom line, they love VA's because they make more money *from you than you make from them, by and large*. Each year, no matter what the market does they get these high fees even if you don't. So why should they care?

I believe that most of the advisors that sell variable annuities are often not fully aware even themselves of the expenses and costs they are selling to people every day. Once, I had a competing advisor in my office that challenged my analysis, only to sit there agog as I unraveled the many layers of fees and charges of his former client's variable annuity.

**If I am displeased with my variable annuity, can I get out of it?**

There are usually 7 to 8 year surrender charge periods for VA's. That means you would have to pay a predetermined charge to surrender the policy within that time frame. However, please note that if you discover your true VA fees and charges are equal to or less than the surrender charges, it may be worth your while to pay the surrender charge, if you are so inclined and have performed your own due diligence before the decision to surrender. For example, if you find your VA fees are 4% per year and your surrender charge to get out of it is 4% or less, then by waiting another 3 to 4 years for the surrender to go away, you will pay that 4% three to four more times more totaling 12-16%. **The longer you stay, the more you pay.** Therefore, it is an illusion to wait for your VA surrender charges to go away if you want out. Waiting could cost you 3 to 4 times as much. Amazing how that works, isn't it?

*Also, I am not telling everyone to surrender their variable annuities, just for the record.*

## LIFETIME INCOME RIDERS AND INCOME PAYOUT OPTIONS

### Are lifetime income riders just like a pension from an employer?

A pension for a retiree from a company is derived from an annuity issued by a life insurance company. Many people do not realize when they have a pension they also have an annuity. They had no say as to where and what type of product is paying out their pension. They are just glad to have it. Pensions are insured by the Pension Benefit Guaranty Corporation (PBGC). In a pension, you elect a settlement and then no longer have access to the principal and cannot change the terms.

When you buy your own private annuity in the open market to be used as a future pension, you never relinquish access to the principal and you can usually get higher payouts than employer-sponsored pensions as well as some additional bells and whistles, such as health care extended benefits.

## What income payout options are available in FIA's and VA's?

By and large, from my experience and research on payouts, I have found that income payout options from FIA's are largely more favorable than income payouts from VA's. Also, many VA income riders do not offer a 100% spousal continuation income stream. VA's often must "annuitize" to pay the income. We call "annuitizing" what it really is, "annuicide." You almost never want to annuitize any contract, because the payout can be very low and you lose control of the principal. Do not confuse a lifetime income rider and annuitization. The confusion lies in the common words used for both such as lifetime. But lifetime income benefit riders pay higher income streams than annuitization settlements. The only exception is an immediate lifetime only annuity on a person who is 85 or older.

When there are two of you, you almost always want to pick 100% joint and survivor income. In this way, when either spouse deceases, the income they have been getting is uninterrupted and continues for the surviving spouse's lifetime.

## Actually where is my money in a VA or FIA?

In a **variable annuity**, your money is not part of the insurance company's general account. Your money is invested in mutual fund clones, technically called sub-accounts. In VA's there is no guarantee of your principal by any entity. If you have an income rider attached, it will encumber the insurance company to pay you out via the conditions of the contract.

In a **fixed or FIA annuity**, your money becomes part of the issuing insurance company's general account. Your funds are not invested in the market. As stated earlier, fixed and fixed indexed annuities (FIA's) are guaranteed insurance contracts (GIC's). These companies are limited to minimal leverage of deposits and many companies have reinsurance agreements with other life insurance companies. There is also a state guaranty fund backup in case of failure. For example, in the

State of Ohio, there is $250,000 of State guaranty money per company per person. The State Guaranty Fund is ironically not truly guaranteed. Its promise is more implied than rigidly stated in case of insurer default.

## A FINAL WORD ABOUT ANNUITIES

In closing, I do not feel annuities are for everyone. Many people can benefit from them, but there are always exceptions where they aren't totally necessary. There are appropriate annuities and inappropriate annuities. Furthermore, there are good financial advisors and poor advisors. Unfortunately, sometimes advisors recommend annuities that are less than suitable for a client. My overall advice is to approach annuities, like any investment, with caution, and make sure you fully understand the terms, costs and conditions before buying.

# CHAPTER 10

# THE SKINNY ON FINDING THE RIGHT ADVISOR

*The advisor you had during the accumulation stage may not be the best advisor for the distribution-preservation stage. The skill sets for the two phases are very different.* ~ Jeff Cirino, EMBA, CFP®

## HOW TO BE CERTAIN YOU FIND AND HIRE THE BEST ADVISOR FOR YOUR UNIQUE FINANCIAL SITUATION.

### Step #1: Don't go it alone

The rules of the retirement planning game are changing rapidly today. You need trusted professionals who focus on solving these types of financial and legal problems. These trusted professionals will not typically be found in the form of your favorite bank teller, nor at the local coffee shop, beauty salon or golf course. The most complete review available will be with a specialized team of professionals, consisting of a qualified estate planning attorney, a CPA, and a CFP®, which is a Certified Financial Planner ™ skilled in asset protection and retirement income planning.

## Step #2: If it sounds too good to be true, it probably is

Unfortunately, it's common today to hear about retirees who have made poor decisions because they bought into a "great opportunity." For instance, if you hear about an account that guarantees anything over 6% when you know darn well the bank down the road is paying 1 to 3% on CDs, you better think twice. That's a giant, waving, red flag. When you hear something that sounds good and you want to believe it, ask more questions like: "So what are the strings attached?" If someone tells you, "No strings," then most likely you need to turn and run. There are many great financial products with attractive features, but even the great opportunities out there come with "rules" (aka "strings attached"). You need to know what they are and if they are acceptable to you and in line with your planning goals. Always use and trust your own good judgment and common sense.

## Step #3: Watch out for Commission Brokers

Do you really know how your advisor is being compensated for the advice he/she is giving you? Furthermore, do you think you have paid an amount equal to the level of service and value you have received? TRANSLATION: Is the fee you are paying worth the advice? Finally, no matter where you park your money in the risk world, it will cost you. You can lower your fees by minimizing risk. However, if you want to lower fees on your risk money, then it is critical for you to know what you are currently paying, so you have a baseline of comparison.

## Step #4: Beware of online "resources"

Information online should be viewed with a very skeptical eye. Today, it is not uncommon for retirees to jump online to do research. The critical question is are you getting information from a credible source? This can be very difficult to decipher online. Information overload is another problem. If you enter the keyword "revocable trust" on Google, you'll come with about 962,000 articles, websites and "resources" to consider. Yes, you need to do research, but on the right things, and you need to know what should be ignored by finding the right help. Focus your due diligence on finding the right planning team to assist you.

### Step #5: Demand Proof!

There's nothing worse than getting sold a bad idea. Slick talk can be very persuasive, but it may prove financially disastrous. When seeking professional advice, we recommend that you assess just how accomplished your potential advice giver really is. How that person answers the following questions should give you a good idea of their qualifications and passion for their work:

## DO YOU INVEST IN YOUR PROFESSIONAL KNOWLEDGE?

This question is a great way to gauge the prospective advisor's commitment to staying current on new laws, tax code changes, product innovations and cutting edge strategies to help preserve and grow your wealth. If you have a large IRA you're considering moving, for example, you might be swayed by knowing if an advisor participates in regular training around the country alongside an elite group of the nation's top financial professionals, staying abreast of the most tax efficient strategies for your particular retirement account. Beware of "financial professionals" who simply pass an exam to become licensed and never commit to ongoing education beyond that point. Financial Advising is an ever-evolving industry, and it may be wise to question the long-term discipline of an advisor who won't commit to staying at the head of his or her class.

## WHERE DO I START LOOKING FOR AN ADVISOR?

One of the best ways to draw from a quality pool of potential advisors is to interview, exclusively, Certified Financial Planners™. Keep in mind, every CFP® professional is not guaranteed to be a 100% right fit for you. Even amongst CFP's, advice can and does vary greatly, so you still have to do your own due diligence. But, being board certified ensures there have been no legal or ethical violations levied on the CFP® you are considering as well as a very high and proven skill level.

As a CFP® professional, one has to go through the education, background check, degree requirement, financial exams, continuing education, and of course, passing the incredibly challenging 2-day exam. The exam covers all investments, tax code mastery, estate planning, economics, insurance, and individual retirement planning mastery.

You see, there really is no financial planning license *per se*. Most new professionals start with a life and annuity license, and they can actually hold themselves out as a financial planner. If one is insurance-only licensed, it is illegal for them to discuss or advise in any way on securities.

An advisor with an insurance license and/or a securities license has only the state and their Broker/Dealer as a reporting entity, which limits recourse for the client if they wish to file a complaint.

**A CFP® which is also a fee-based financial advisor offers three layers of oversight for the protection of clients:**

1. For securities, a fee-based advisor is bound by the state of domicile's Securities Division or the SEC if they manage over $100 million. <u>The absence of commissions eliminates potential conflicts of interest.</u>

2. Registered investment advisory firms or RIA's, are held to the higher "fiduciary" level of responsibility for clients as opposed to commissioned brokers.

   A fiduciary is one that will be held to the standard of 'always do what's best for the client.'

3. A CFP® must answer to the CFP Board of Standards. A CFP® professional can only keep the letters of CFP® as long as there are no ethical or legal violations and records ongoing continuing education.

So the question comes down to whether or not you want your doctor to be board certified or not? Many are not. That is a scary thought. Then, why would you want to work with a financial advisor who is not board certified? Your money is as nearly as important as your health.

## SOME FINAL THOUGHTS

I would like to end this book with some snippets of truth to help you regain control of your money.

1. Ask the 5 questions from chapter 1 to every advisor going forward, when you are given a formal recommendation. Be sure to make them answer in plain language as well.

2. If you own mutual funds and/or variable annuities, you should have a third-party advisor calculate all of the costs, fees, and charges. Make sure they show you with a third-party source and show you how they arrived at the total costs.

3. Keep your cost of capital low. Costs kill. They are not necessary, and actually are quite detrimental.

4. Know the taxability of your investments. A CFP® professional or a CPA can easily explain the tax treatment of your various accounts.

5. Know the difference between what is a risk investment and a safe investment.

6. Make sure you know how much risk you have, especially if you're over 50.

7. Demand 100% transparency in where and how your money is invested, as well as 100% disclosure of an advisor's fee or commission compensation. If they can't answer it and explain it genuinely, then run. If they are not open about that or they lie about it, then what else will they lie about?

8. In general, avoid variable annuities, especially for IRA's. You do not need insurance costs on your IRA.

9. Fixed and Fixed Indexed Annuities should never be confused with Variable Annuities. They are completely different animals and unfortunately they share the same categorical name "annuity."

10. Make sure you understand that markets make money; advisors and fund managers, myself included, DON'T. Don't fight the efficiency of the markets.

11. Don't let the Wall Street "Great and Powerful Oz" personas make you think they are smarter than you. They cannot predict the market or stock moves either.

12. Stock picking and market timing is inconsistent and more akin to casino gambling than anything else.

13. Don't chase mutual fund track records. A good year or two only means that asset class just so happened to do well. When you chase returns, you get burned. Plain and simple.

14. Don't allow advisors or salespeople to pressure you or rush you. An intelligent, prudent advisor will work at your pace in your plan development. If you have pressure exerted on you by an advisor they are either in need of money or not thinking about what you think.

15. Work with a team of professionals, such as an Estate Planner, CPA, and CFP®. Don't work with insurance only advisors for your total planning needs. They are missing a whole other world of expertise, and advice will be one-sided.

16. Diversity is the only 'free lunch' in finance. With optimal diversity, you normally have greater upside and lesser downside over time.

17. Indexing with Exchange Traded Funds offers transparency, diversity, and decent tax-efficiency. They should be examined before they are dismissed.

18. If your advisor is not really listening to you and is just focusing on the sale. Make him listen to this…"Goodbye!"

19. Don't make the mistake of giving up on trying to improve your financial decisions. There really are a lot of people out there willing to educate you before they offer recommendations. Don't be discouraged by your past experiences, just be wiser from them.

20. For your equity management, use fee-based over commission-based advice and management. You pay more with commission and you run a high risk that they will stop caring about you after they get all your assets under their wing. They have to hunt new game with fresh commissions to feed their families.

I hope you take away even a few of the snippets I have written about in this book. I just want you all to know how much I appreciate your time taken to read this book. By reading books like "The Skinny," it says you are ready to continue on your quest for making better-informed decisions and you recognize that the *status quo* you know may not be the best for you anymore.

I have only the best of wishes for investors. I want you to know my intent stems from the passionate desire to be the voice of reason. After having personally subscribed to all of the Wall Street lies and myths, but have lived to tell about it, I cannot tell you how much it has ticked me off all these years to hear some of the falsehoods people share with me about their own advisor experiences.

Go forward and demand more transparency, added value, and sensible advice from your financial professional and any new ones you may be interviewing. You are now armed with many tools to make better-informed financial decisions going forward.

I hope you can appreciate the passion and fire I have for my profession and I hope you recognize my sincere desire to uncover financial deception. Don't let the Wall Street bullies make you think they know something you can't know. They are dead wrong. Not everyone will agree with my assessments, and that is fine. There are always differing views, but that is what makes free enterprise and America so great.

I wish you all a long, healthy, and prosperous life.

Feel free to e-mail me with questions or comments at: jeff@alphaplanners.com

# CHAPTER 11

# EPILOGUE

Before we say goodbye and have a good life, I would like to share with you a few final thoughts on "Financial Coaching." Coaching is in addition to financial advising.

As I have stated in previous chapters, market timing and stock picking do not work, except by luck. Our markets are so efficient, it is a fool's errand to try to outwit and predict the future of a stock, an industry, a market, or an entire global economy.

Furthermore, asset allocation and investment expenses are the two areas that affect your money most. Even when someone does attain an efficient portfolio, especially if their mind about money is twisted or based on myths, they will intervene at the worst possible time and wreck their long-term goals. This is where the need for a coach becomes apparent. A coach should be able to regularly reinforce solid academic principals of long-term investing. A coach should also be able to show you how to not listen to the financial media. A financial coach should also have regular contact with you on a monthly basis. A combination of group meetings and one-on-ones can suffice nicely.

Most importantly, a coach can teach you what things to ignore, and which things to which you should be tethered. A financial coach is someone whom you trust but verify. Remember folks, 98% of the financial world is out for your money. Some are willing to go to great lengths to do anything to get your money. Be careful. Use your rational mind and trust your gut when you have no other way to measure a situation.

My hope is that all of you get back control of your money, don't fall for scare tactics, and when someone is pressuring you... leave.

After all, this is YOUR money, YOUR future and YOUR American dream.

CPSIA information can be obtained at www.ICGtesting.com
Printed in the USA
BVOW08*1952090416

443412BV00001B/3/P

9 780989 518734